Money Guy

The Education of a Political Fundraiser

Robert A. Farmer
with Chris Black

outskirtspress
DENVER, COLORADO

The opinions expressed in this manuscript are solely the opinions of the author and do not represent the opinions or thoughts of the publisher. The author has represented and warranted full ownership and/or legal right to publish all the materials in this book.

The Money Guy
The Education of a Political Fundraiser
All Rights Reserved.
Copyright © 2014 Robert A. Farmer
v2.0

Cover Photo © 2014 JupiterImages Corporation. All rights reserved - used with permission.

This book may not be reproduced, transmitted, or stored in whole or in part by any means, including graphic, electronic, or mechanical without the express written consent of the publisher except in the case of brief quotations embodied in critical articles and reviews.

Outskirts Press, Inc.
http://www.outskirtspress.com

Paperback ISBN: 978-1-4787-1897-0
Hardback ISBN: 978-1-4787-2136-9

Outskirts Press and the "OP" logo are trademarks belonging to Outskirts Press, Inc.

PRINTED IN THE UNITED STATES OF AMERICA

To my wonderful grandchildren: Robert, Emily and Melanie.
May each of you realize the promise of America.

Contents

Chapter 1: The Money Guy 1
Chapter 2: The First Lessons 23
Chapter 3: Only in America 46
Chapter 4: A New Beginning 65
Chapter 5: The Father of Soft Money 97
Chapter 6: The Rainmaker 126
Chapter 7: Living in Paradise 151
Chapter 8: The Final Campaigns 175
Epilogue 209

CHAPTER 1

The Money Guy

The limousine doors closed with a thump and I turned to John B. Anderson, a Republican Congressman from Illinois who was running for President of the United States in 1980.

The red and blue emergency lights of police cars and motorcycles flashed ahead of us. A long line of vehicles lined up behind the limo including a van for the Secret Service agents, another one for campaign staff and a third for the traveling press corps. A police cruiser took up the rear as a kind of caboose. The candidate and I were sandwiched in a security blanket. The Secret Service agent who told me where to sit before closing the door, hopped into the front passenger seat. Seconds later, the motorcade pulled away from Logan International Airport in Boston on its way to my home in nearby Brookline.

I had flown into Logan and made this same trip to my house at 540 Chestnut Hill Avenue countless times. Normally, the trip took about 40 minutes because of Boston's notorious heavy traffic and stop lights. On this day, the motorcade took off like a bullet and sped through the tunnel that runs beneath Boston Harbor, up the Southeast Expressway, down Storrow Drive to Kenmore Square, to Boylston Street to Brookline and my home at 540 Chestnut Hill Avenue. The nine mile trip took ten minutes flat.

The motorcade moved at top speed ignoring red lights and stop signs. Pedestrians paused on sidewalks and gawked at the motorcade with open mouths. Boston and then Brookline police cruisers stopped traffic at every intersection. I can no longer remember what Anderson and I discussed in the comfortable cocoon of the back seat of the limo. But I will never forget the exhilaration and excitement of my first motorcade ride. I had no idea at the time, but it would be the first of many over the next 30 years.

After graduating from Dartmouth College and Harvard Law School, I enjoyed some success in business. I founded and built my own educational publishing company. The Anderson campaign, a quixotic national run by a long shot candidate, launched me onto a second improbable career as a political fundraiser. For the next 30 years, I claimed a seat at the table of American politics as The Money Guy.

Fundraising is essential in politics. It has often been called ``the first primary" in presidential campaigns. Jesse M. Unruh, the state treasurer of California, once said, ``Money is the mother's milk of politics." And Mark Hanna, the legendary political boss from my hometown of Cleveland,

THE MONEY GUY

Ohio, said, "There are two things that are important in politics. The first is money ...and I can't remember what the second one is." Hanna is considered the father of modern fundraisers. He hit up his rich pals for William McKinley, the Republican Governor of Ohio, and got his friend elected to the presidency twice over the golden throated William Jennings Bryan.

Money is the first thing that you can count. Early public opinion polls are meaningless because they only measure name recognition. Endorsements mean little because many establishment candidates with dozens of big name endorsements go nowhere. Remember President Ed Muskie? Ed Muskie, a Democratic Senator from Maine, was the insider candidate expected to cinch the presidential nomination in 1972. George McGovern, powered by an anti war movement, won the nomination. Muskie withdrew early in the race in April.

Of course, money is not everything. The candidate needs to be the right person for the right time and the issues are important. But money accounts for a lot. The press focuses on money because money is real. A campaign cannot lie about money.

I have always enjoyed the fundraising side of campaigns because every month your boss, the candidate, knows in measurable terms whether or not you are doing a good job. The campaign's political director does not know if he made the right calls until Election Day. The press secretary lives and dies with every story and news cycle. In every

THE MONEY GUY

presidential campaign I have been in, the first campaign manager did not survive until the end of the campaign.

But everyone knows right away if the finance chair or the money guy is succeeding or failing. Every day and every event shows results or not. In every presidential campaign, a candidate is going to experience setbacks and lose some primaries and his or her ability to soldier on depends upon the availability of resources. Nobody ever dropped out of a presidential campaign for any reason other than they ran out of funds and could no longer afford to keep a plane in the air. I remember being on a private flight with Bill Clinton asking him what was the only known cure for presidential fever. He shrugged his shoulders. I said, ``Formaldehyde.'' He was not particularly amused.

Candidates who cannot raise enough money to pass the threshold of viability never get out of the starting gate. It is not easy to raise millions of dollars for a political campaign and, with few exceptions, every candidate I have met in life hates it. Politicians like to ask for votes but they do not like to ask for a check. But I liked it and turned out to be pretty good at dialing for dollars for men and women in whom I believed.

I was absolutely stunned and flattered when The Boston Globe described me as ``rookie of the year, fundraising division'' for my work for Anderson. It was quite a compliment for a political outsider and newcomer to politics. When that column ran in the Boston Globe, it struck me that I had worked in business for many years and never once seen my name in the newspaper. Politics was a whole different arena. Everything is played out on the public stage. During Michael Dukakis' presidential campaign in 1988, I received 20 calls from news reporters every day. Everything ended up in the public realm. By contrast, most people in business, even the successful well known corporate CEO's, work in relative privacy. Their decisions and day to day operational activities are rarely subject to any public scrutiny.

Between 1980 and 2010, I was the National Treasurer for the presidential campaigns of John Glenn, Michael Dukakis, Bill Clinton and John Kerry. I also raised money for the presidential campaigns of Walter Mondale, Dick Gephardt and Barack Obama as well as dozens of House and Senate candidates and gubernatorial candidates. In between presidential campaigns, I did a turn as the treasurer for the Democratic National Committee and the Democratic Governors' Association.

I was surprised again when the New York Times dubbed me ``The Father of Soft Money" because of the success of the Dukakis presidential campaign in raising money in $100,000 checks for the Democratic National Committee. In 1988, it was legal to ask wealthy contributors for that kind of money for the national party. The party then assumed responsibility for a portion of the national coordinated campaign for the entire Democratic ticket. While it was allowed by law, no one had ever done it before. I remember the Republican Party poobahs mocked us for this strategy

THE MONEY GUY

in the press. But less than six weeks later, the Republican National Committee was doing the exact same thing.

Back then my personal Rolodex of names and numbers was very slim. My golf and card playing cronies were primarily Republicans. I did not personally know dozens of wealthy Democrats so from the start, I realized I could not necessarily ask for the money myself but I could recruit those who would. Everyone has a personal social and business network and everyone can raise a little bit of money. By pulling all of those individuals into the campaign, the impact was magnified and we built a fundraising organization second to none.

To me, fundraising was all about empowering people and making each individual feel he or she had a stake in the campaign and in our democratic form of government. My good friend Mark Gorenberg, the managing director of Hummer Windblad Venture Partners, a major venture capital firm, recalls the very first fundraiser he ever attended, an event to help Senator John Kerry of Massachusetts retire debt from his 1996 Senate campaign. The event was held at the home of Eric Schmidt, the chairman and CEO of Google, who was a friend of Marks Schmidt said, ``Welcome to political fundraising, the gift that keeps on taking.'' Mark later served as the fundraising chair for California for Kerry's presidential campaign in 2004 and he did a remarkable job.

During this second career, I made wonderful friends, met thousands of extremely successful professionals, slept overnight in the White House and learned a lot about human nature and politics.

The Internet and social media changed the game of fundraising in some fundamental ways. But some things about fundraising never change and can be applied to other fundraising tasks for non-profit organizations and charities. I am writing this book to recount the lessons of successful fundraising for others to use and apply to the causes in which they believe and to share a remarkable and unique American experience of watching presidential politics from the political dugout for three decades.

I learned that fundraising is very personal and people like to be asked. I learned that honesty is always the best policy and it is critical to keep your word. I discovered that no one likes to say no to a request, particularly when it is made in person, and from a friend or colleague. I learned the value of making people feel involved with titles and flattery and recognition. To me, Alice Roosevelt Longworth was wrong. The President's daughter and House Speaker's wife was a legendary wit in Washington. She once famously said, `` If you have something bad to say about someone sit down right next to me." I learned that it is more useful and effective to make friends rather than enemies and idle gossip can destroy a relationship faster than anything. I met some of the most compelling public figures active in American politics in the last part of the 20th century and discovered that they are nothing like you and me but sometimes they are just like the rest of us. And finally, I learned a lesson my mother taught me which is that family is everything, true friends are precious and you want to keep those people whom you can rely upon at the worst of times very close to you.

Asking someone to write a check for a politician is not that difficult. It takes a certain amount of self-confidence, acute sensitivity to the individual and what makes him or her tick, passion for the candidate or cause and relentless persistence and patience. Being a salesman means not taking it personally when someone says no. I can remember the disappointment I felt in business when a proposal was rejected. I would stay late in the office that day making more phone calls because I wanted to end the day and go home on a successful positive note. I hated to lose.

I discovered I had a knack for raising money. I liked people and I enjoyed the process of getting to know enough about them to persuade them to join my cause. I learned something from every single campaign. While some people may be disillusioned with modern politics, I am not. I admire the men and women who run for public office. I came to know the candidates I supported as people as well as politicians. Living in the public eye can be a wrenching experience. There is no privacy and everyone from the loftiest corporate CEO to the common cab driver second guesses everything you do. Our democracy works because leaders are willing to pay the personal price, put themselves out front and lead. I admire those who show the fortitude and courage to plunge into the political fray.

I was thrilled to have the chance to help some of them succeed.

I was an unlikely Democratic Party fundraiser. I was born into a Republican household in Cleveland, Ohio in 1938. When I first saw John Anderson during a televised Republican debate from Iowa, I was a semi-retired 41 year old businessman who did a few hours of work in the morning at my publishing business but spent the rest of the day golfing and playing gin rummy working up to the cocktail hour and a good stiff Scotch. My business was well established by 1980 and required little hands on attention from me. I had an excellent staff of employees. In hindsight, I suspect it was always my goal to be semi-retired. Work was a means to an end. Business was a way to make money so I could do what I really wanted to do which was golfing, playing cards and enjoying a drink with friends.

That is not to say I was lazy. I created my business when I was still in law school. After my first two years at Harvard Law, I was nominated by Dean Erwin Griswold who later served as Solicitor General under Presidents Lyndon B. Johnson and Richard M. Nixon to participate in an honors program sponsored by the Office of Regional Counsel of the Internal Revenue Service. At the time, I wanted to be a tax attorney. I was sent to the IRS regional office in Omaha, Nebraska. Many of the attorneys there were active in the Army Reserve and I decided to sign up. On my 24th birthday in 1962, I reported to Fort Leonard Wood in Missouri for basic training. For the next six weeks, I experienced the extremes of Missouri weather, conditions that alternately afflicted me and my fellow enlistees with sunstroke and frostbite. The enlistment committed me to six years of reserve duty. I had thought I would hate the experience but it turned out just the opposite. I made several lifelong friends and, as someone who grew up in a privileged background of prep schools and Ivy League colleges, I really enjoyed the camaraderie and shared hardship with my fellow reservists. I will never forget one of my bunkmates made the observation the first morning as we stood around waiting for chow that if he had been home right then, he'd be milking cows.

When I returned to Cleveland after basic training, I spent the summer working for a large law firm and got an offer from Ernst & Ernst, then a major Cleveland based accounting firm and a forerunner of Ernst & Young, one of the big four auditing firms, to write manuals on international taxation for foreign countries. The assignment appealed to me and I moved to New York at the end of the summer with the intention of finishing my last year of law school at night at NYU.

Working fulltime and going to class at night took more effort and energy than I expected, however, and I worked for Ernst & Ernst for a year before returning to Harvard Law for my third and final year of school. I have always deeply admired people with the ability to work fulltime during the day and earn an academic degree at night. That type of dedication and stamina takes a special person. I returned to Cambridge with a contract to continue to produce international tax guides. I had done the first one on Germany and developed a template. I borrowed $1,000 in seed money from my father and posted an advertisement on the bulletin board at Harvard for part time workers and hired classmates at $2 an hour. I produced six more tax guides for other countries at a cost of $230 apiece including the typing and sold them for $2,100 each. The guides included a general overview of the country and some tips for businessman on local business practices. By 1965, I had produced tax guides for 80 countries. By graduation day, I realized I had earned more money in school than most graduates earn with years of labor after graduation and I thought I might be onto something .

But I wasn't really sure if this would turn out to be a real business over the long haul so I applied to Harvard Business School at the same time as my younger brother, Brent, who had just graduated from Princeton. My father had also attended the business school. One day, my mother opened a letter from the Dean of Harvard Business School which said, ``Congratulations …your son has just been accepted at HBS." She called my father very excitedly and said Brent had been accepted at the business school. My father asked her to read him the letter but when she finished, he noted that the letter did not say which son was accepted. Two of us had applied so he called the Dean and learned both of us were accepted.

Brent and I started Harvard Business School at the same

time in 1965 but my little side business on tax pamphlets took up so much time, I dropped out after one semester. In fact, I was traveling to New York so much and missing so many classes that my classmates burst into spontaneous applause one day when I actually showed up for a class wearing a business suit and carrying a suitcase. But Harvard Business School gave me an idea for an expansion of my publishing business. I came up with the notion of taking the Harvard Business School curriculum and putting it into self study books. My company Education for Management was born with help from one of my classmates who went to work at a major New York banking investment firm. He helped raise $350,000 in 1968 to launch the company. The business grew like topsy. By the time I sold the business in 1983, it was doing $11 million a year in sales all through direct mail and personal contact.

By that time, I had become deeply involved in political fundraising for Democratic candidates. This was a little more unusual than it appeared. Not only was I a nominal Republican but I was also gay. I did not broadcast that fact. My close friends knew I was gay. I lived with Tim McNeill, who is now the publisher and CEO of Wisdom Publications, the U.S. publisher of the Dalai Lama, who was my partner at the time. Being gay was not accepted the way it is today. Until 1973, the American Psychiatric Association described homosexuality as a mental disorder. When I was young, I hoped being gay was a phase and one day I would wake up and be heterosexual. So I kept my sexual preferences private and maintained a policy of discretion in the business world.

Indeed, my card playing buddies did not know I was gay for years and I never told my parents until much later. My brothers did not know until I was able to finally accept that this was the way I am when I was in my mid-30's.

Social change takes time and politics can be as conventional and tradition bound as business. While the world was changing for women and minorities, the typical Presidential candidate, typical Senate candidate, typical gubernatorial candidate in 1980 was still a white middle-aged heterosexual man with a lovely wife, a couple of kids and a really nice dog.

For example, Gerry Studds, an enormously popular Congressman who represented Cape Cod in Massachusetts for many years, won election to his 10th district seat in 1972 but did not publically disclose he was gay until 1983. Barney Frank, another Massachusetts Congressman, did not come out publically until 1987. In fact, both were forced out of the closet because of scandals. Studds was involved with congressional pages and Frank was friendly with a gay hustler who ran his business out of Barney's apartment without Barney's knowledge. In those days, gay men often came out of the closet kicking and screaming because of indiscretions. As recently as 2004, a closeted gay man was governor of New Jersey, James McGreevey. When forced out because of a scandal involving a state employee, his lovely wife appeared to be as shocked as everyone else. So politics did not seem exactly welcoming to a gay man at that time.

Tim McNeill and I were home in Brookline watching TV

◄ THE MONEY GUY

when John Anderson came to my attention. I was not active politically but I considered myself a Republican because my family had been Republican. Politics was not a big part of my life. I was not ideological but I considered myself a moderate Main Street Republican. Tim was the opposite. He was a progressive Democrat from New York, a former Peace Corps volunteer and a graduate of the John F. Kennedy School of Government at Harvard. He has always said that Anderson represented a middle ground candidate we could both support. Anderson's straightforward candor impressed us. When other candidates dodged the question of what they most regretted in their lives, Anderson said he wished he could take back his vote in favor of the Gulf of Tonkin Resolution in 1964. That resolution gave President Johnson almost unlimited power to escalate the war in Vietnam. I thought Anderson showed guts to come right out and admit he had been wrong. After the debate ended, I wrote a $1,000 check to Anderson, the largest amount allowed by law to a candidate for federal office in 1980. And I convinced a close friend to write a check as well. It was the second political contribution I had ever made in my life. The first went to President Nixon, another moderate Republican.

That check got me invited to a meeting of other Anderson supporters in a conference room at an investment banking firm in downtown Boston. During the meeting, I suggested Anderson might raise money through direct mail. Direct mail is a very effective marketing technique that marries advertising and sales. With direct mail, a seller sends a message directly to a buyer sidestepping any middleman and tailoring the pitch to the individual. In my view, this technique worked effectively whether you were selling books or a candidate.

After I made some comments about direct marketing, David Thorne, another Anderson supporter at the meeting, suggested I should be finance chairman of the Anderson campaign in Massachusetts. David is a remarkably gracious and sophisticated man who has been successful in publishing, consulting, real estate and financial services. He is also one of the closest friends of John F. Kerry who was then a lawyer in private practice in Boston but a few years later won election as a U.S. Senator from Massachusetts. Thorne and Kerry were classmates at Yale, served in Vietnam in the Navy together, and became active in Vietnam Veterans against the War. Kerry was married for many years to David's twin sister, Julia. President Barack Obama named David ambassador to Italy in 2009. By then, Senator Kerry was the powerful chairman of the Senate Committee on Foreign Relations. David spent much of his childhood in Italy and speaks fluent Italian. Obama made a great choice in naming him ambassador.

By appointing me finance chairman of John Anderson's Massachusetts campaign, essentially by acclamation, David Thorne set in motion the next phase of my life. I was eager to take on this challenge. The campaign came along at a time when I was facing the realization that being semi-retired at age 41 may not have been the most fulfilling of lifestyles. I was bored and restless. Tim threw a surprise party for my 40th birthday and remembers I seemed very depressed afterwards. I thought I should have done a lot more with my life than I had at that major milestone. So I was clearly ready to embrace a new purpose and cause.

After that preliminary meeting I began to put into action my idea of using direct contact to raise money for Anderson. I called the national Anderson headquarters in Washington and asked for the name of every Massachusetts person who had sent $100 or more to the campaign. There were 400 people. I then offered to host a $100 per person fundraising event at my house and asked the campaign to find a date on his schedule, perhaps when Anderson was flying through Boston on his way to campaign in New Hampshire. It was arranged. I then called the first 100 names on the list and asked each one if he or she would agree to be named on the invitation as a co-host of the fundraiser. Their only commitment would be to try and bring three or four other people to the event although I indicated the campaign would certainly appreciate another contribution. Ninety of the 100 agreed. We were also creating a finance committee for Anderson in Massachusetts. I invited each to join the committee and many did. That committee turned into yet another social network.

I was running out of time, so I sent a letter to the other 300 and asked the same question. About 45 of the 300 agreed to be a co-host. (I was not yet aware of the value of phone banks to make dozens of phone calls.) While a 15 percent response rate is excellent in direct mail, I couldn't help but be struck by the discrepancy. When I talked to potential givers, I got a 90 percent response. When I wrote to them, I got a 15 percent response. I learned my first lesson in political fundraising. All fundraising is personal. During a personal phone call, I established a rapport with each person. We all had something in common; we liked John Anderson and we all liked him enough to contribute to his campaign. During a phone conversation, I would introduce myself and tell a bit about my background and ask the Anderson supporter about himself and his work and his family.. People love to talk about themselves. For highly motivated political supporters, a letter might be enough, but I discovered closing a deal with most people took a personal connection.

In 1980 Anderson lost the Republican nomination to Ronald Reagan, the former actor and governor of California who went on to change the face of American politics during his eight year presidency. Anderson had begun his career as a conservative but evolved into a moderate Rockefeller Republican by 1980. But that campaign showed very clearly that the base of the GOP was turning more and more conservative and Reagan became the apotheosis of conservatism in the Grand Old Party.

I hadn't reflected much on my own personal views over the years. I was a Republican the same way I was Bob Farmer, it was not a choice so much as a birthright. I came from a classic Main Street, Chamber of Commerce, and

THE MONEY GUY

country club kind of background where everyone was a Republican. Republicanism to me meant Dwight D. Eisenhower and Nelson Rockefeller and Richard Nixon, moderates all. Tim McNeill is convinced that his progressive inclinations pulled me towards the left. We lived in a very liberal community and Tim was very concerned with the plight of the poor and displaced dating back to his three years working in Afghanistan in the Peace Corps. He definitely influenced me. Tim and I had sponsored two Vietnamese brothers who fled Communism and were living in a refugee camp in Malaysia. I drew a great deal of satisfaction out of helping those young men realize the promise of America. Each became an American citizen and both are very successful today.

Anderson decided to run in the general election as an independent. President Jimmy Carter had beaten back a primary challenge from Senator Edward M. Kennedy, the senior Senator from Massachusetts, and been renominated on the Democratic side. My Democratic friends in Massachusetts were bitterly disappointed by Kennedy's loss and disliked Carter. Anderson had the potential to draw a lot of those votes from liberal Democrats who just could not stomach Jimmy Carter. In the general election in November 1980, Anderson won 5.7 million votes, barely seven percent of the votes cast. (He did much better in my adopted state of Massachusetts where he won 15 percent of the vote, enough to split the progressive vote and allow Reagan to carry the liberal state over Carter by about 4,000 votes.) It was the best showing nationally by a third party candidate since George Wallace, the former Alabama governor and segregationist and his 14 percent showing in 1968. But more important, by getting more than 5 percent of the vote, Anderson was eligible for federal matching funds of some of his contributions. This proved to be the key to my second lesson in politics.

Anderson was undone by his big proposal in favor of a 50 cent increase in the federal gas tax. He was not wrong. His position reflected an early recognition of the United States' dangerous dependence on foreign oil. The theory was the higher the price of gasoline, the lower the consumption, a pattern seen in European countries which impose extraordinarily high taxes on gasoline. But Americans love their automobiles and hate taxes and by November, Democrats had reluctantly returned to the Carter fold and Ronald Reagan won the election with the help of so-called Reagan Democrats and the independent vote.

I had an idea when Anderson was still at 25 percent in public opinion polls earlier in the year of asking supporters to loan money to the campaign and then get it back when the candidate got the federal matching funds after the election. I sent a letter from the campaign to every Massachusetts' Anderson contributor who had given at least $200 and asked them to loan whatever they could spare to the campaign up to the legal limit of $1,000. In the letter, I promised the campaign would pay them back if Anderson got more than 5 percent in the election and qualified for the matching funds.

◄ **THE MONEY GUY**

The response was amazing. Every day in the mail, I got stacks of return envelopes containing checks. It was so successful the Washington headquarters asked me to take the loan program national. I drafted a letter sent out to supporters across the United States signed by me with a contract for the loan terms. I included my home phone number because I believed the fact I was willing to give out my home phone number sent an important message. Most direct mail solicitations never include a home phone number from an executive. I wanted them to understand I was so committed that I was willing to give out my home phone number. The response again was overwhelming. Every day was like Christmas when the postman arrived. I took the checks and sent them overnight to Washington via Federal Express. That money kept John Anderson on the road and in the hunt for the rest of the campaign.

After the election, I got a call from the Washington headquarters saying a number of campaign advisers were submitting bills for their services after the fact to take advantage of the windfall of federal matching funds and did I want to submit a bill for my services because they intended to use the matching funds to pay off staff and vendors. I immediately was concerned that there would be no money left to pay back the thousands of people who had loaned the candidate money at my request. I was also shocked that the campaign staff apparently had no intention of honoring that promise. I was probably still a little naïve about politics back then. This had been my first involvement and I made assumptions that may have reflected my own personal code of conduct.

In this instance, I felt strongly my personal reputation and word of honor was at stake. I had signed the letter asking for the loans and promised each of those donors they would be paid back after the election if John Anderson won enough votes to reach the threshold for matching funds. Anderson was out of town on vacation with his wife but I tracked him down. I told him that the people who financed his campaign believed in him and worked and sacrificed to send that money. It was real money for him and real money for them. Anderson was surprised, shocked and indignant. He agreed with me and made certain that every single nickel was paid back. I never took a penny and never asked for a penny. I learned another lesson in that campaign, you keep promises.

John Anderson and his wife Kiki became close friends during that campaign. Although he did not win the election, he made a difference in that campaign and showed that a Congressman with a few good ideas and a lot of drive could seek the highest office in the land and inspire millions of people. I found it a heady experience to be involved in the pursuit of power at that level. Politics, to me, was meaningful. Elections matter. I may not have paid a lot of attention to politics as a young man but I came to appreciate acutely as I grew older of how much public policy affects our civil liberties and our quality of life. As a gay man, I was fortunate to be protected to some degree from overt discrimination because I enjoyed some financial success early in life and I traveled in tolerant circles. However, not everyone is so fortunate.

When an individual gives money to a candidate, that person is taking a leap of faith. The donor wants the candidate to win but the support involves more than that. Writing a check, attending a fundraising event, calling friends to back the candidate are all ways the donor expresses hope. Nothing is more American than that.

By the time the election took place in November 1980, I was hooked on politics. I had never been a bashful person and I liked people. I met many new people, all of them with interesting stories and many with impressive accomplishments, through the Anderson campaign. Politics changed my whole life. I was establishing a connection with people and developed a social life that had me going out to dinner nearly every night of the week. All the energy I had focused on becoming a business success was now channeled into my new avocation. I flunked retirement and began working harder than I ever had before on raising money for political candidates, a ``job'' I would do as a volunteer for the next 30 years. I was about to head out on the biggest adventure of my life.

CHAPTER 2

The First Lessons

As the Anderson motorcade pulled into Chestnut Hill Avenue for the first political fundraiser I ever hosted, I immediately noticed dozens of automobiles parked along the sides of the street. The town of Brookline, Massachusetts forbids on-street overnight parking so it unusual to see many cars parked on the street even during the early evening hours when guests might be visiting a neighbor for drinks and dinner.

On this day, cars lined the streets for blocks around my house. There were so many cars that the local police were on the scene directing traffic. All those unfamiliar cars were my first sign that the event would be a success. The Secret Service had reserved space for the motorcade so we pulled up right to the front door. I wasn't completely relieved yet but I could feel myself relaxing just a little.

I cannot count the number of fundraising cocktail parties, breakfasts, lunches, dinners and meet the candidate sessions I have hosted over the years. Yet it never fails that I am always seized by a cold panic in the final minutes before the start time for fear no one will show up. The fact that this has never happened does not make a bit of difference. I still worry the very same way I worried before that first Anderson event in Brookline.

I'm told that famous well-established actors experience similar pre-show butterflies. The event is show time for me and I take care to prepare carefully but the jitters always show up at the last minute. For me the scene never varies: The caterer puts hors d'oeuvres into the oven to heat and arranges platters of carefully crafted delicacies for the guests. The bartender puts out the ice, sets up the bar, and opens the first bottles of wine. The tables are set beautifully with candles and flowers. The wait staff stands at attention. Everything is ready and I die a thousand deaths wondering if this is the night I will be hugely embarrassed because no one will show up.

Campaign advance people learn early on to schedule campaign events in small venues to make the crowd look bigger. Shoehorning hundreds of people into a very small hall generates a sense of excitement and makes the campaign look as though public support is building. There is considerable risk to pulling this stunt with fundraisers, however. Donors are usually well-to-do people with expectations. Coming to an event is an inconvenience for most of them. They expect a decent drink, good food and a nice atmosphere. Being jammed into a hot meeting hall with huge lines at

THE FIRST LESSONS

the bar and nothing to eat but stale crackers and tasteless cheese is no way to treat contributors. Contributors want to mingle, chat with friends and acquaintances, maybe meet a few new people, definitely meet and chat with the candidate, listen to a very short speaking program and get out in a timely way.

Political contributors always welcome face time with the candidate. Candidates understand this and most of them make a genuine effort to be ``on'' for contributors, to listen to their concerns, to deliver a strong enthusiastic call to arms and to thank them profusely for their support. I find it amusing to watch guests jockey for face time with the candidate. Even the wealthiest most successful businessman gets a kick out of chatting with the man or woman who might be the next President of the United States. There are not a lot of things even a powerful politician can do for a successful wealthy individual. Rich people can buy what they want and need. Contrary to what many people think, politicians make little difference to the quality of life of the truly rich. The one thing a politician **can** give is a bit of attention and time. I have met very few donors who did not take great delight with a personal chat with a future President and who did not prize the classic Grip and Grin photograph taken at the fundraiser and who could not repeat the conversation verbatim years later.

I have my own ``brag wall'' at my condo in Florida. I have filled the long hallway with photographs of me and all of the politicians I worked for over the past 30 years. When

THE MONEY GUY

I show it to friends, I tell them that not one of the many people shown on the wall have a single picture of me on their walls. I call it my ``I love Bob wall''.

Fundraisers not only like to be acknowledged but they like to get credit for helping. There is a story, probably apocryphal but too good not to tell about a labor union boss who allegedly wrote a $50,000 check to the Democratic National Committee. He first went to the Majority Leader's Office and said that he was writing this check because of him. He then went to the Speaker's office and made the same statement. Then he visited the Chairman of the party.... made the same statement.... and handed him the check. Essentially he was earning three chits with these important leaders with one check. Not a bad strategy if you're looking for credit.

Our house in Brookline proved to be an excellent spot for fundraising. For the Anderson event, we draped the house with bunting and set up a speaker system in the backyard. We transformed the grounds into a campaign rally site. John Anderson is not a tall man so we found a small box for him to stand on. I introduced him as `` the next President of the United States''. It was a bit overwhelming to say those words in my own backyard. It was the first time I had ever introduced a presidential candidate and it would not be the last.

The United States of America is the oldest democracy in the world and you hear a lot of complaints these days about how vested interests and money play a disproportionate

THE FIRST LESSONS

role in public policy. I cannot disagree with that conclusion. I have come to believe the necessity of raising money and the extraordinary amount of time it takes are counterproductive to good government. Members of Congress spend too much time dialing for dollars, time better spent studying issues and holding hearings and tending to the people's business. Senators and House members cannot make a fundraising call from a government office so many of them dash from their official offices to a hideaway office somewhere on Capitol Hill or perhaps a boiler room set up by the national committees to take time out of their busy days and make phone calls to potential givers. No sooner does a successful candidate take public office than the cycle begins again. More than one office holder has told me how oppressive they find the burden of raising funds for campaigns. I find that distressing. It is a huge waste of an important official's time but too many spend too many hours doing just that to raise the money they need or think they need to win election or reelection.

In our system, there is a correlation between money and influence and I saw it many times as a fundraiser and, for two years, as a rainmaker for one of Washington's biggest lobbying firms, Cassidy & Associates. It would be excessively cynical and incorrect to say that all politicians can be bought and sold like commodities. But some can. I remember vividly one finance committee meeting for a very senior member of the United States Senate in the 1980's. A number of public policy issues were discussed but the Senator was only interested in how his position

◄ THE MONEY GUY

would affect his reelection. He did not consider the public good, only his personal political fortunes. It was an eye opening meeting for me.

More than one donor has flat out asked for a commitment or favor in return for a donation. It is illegal to do favors for money and everyone knows it but I have been surprised by the boldness and sense of entitlement of some people.

One time during John Glenn's presidential campaign in 1984, I met with a very prominent businessman in a southern state. ``Mistah Farmah,'' he said in a thick southern accent. ``I can raise half a million dollars for you. But …I'd like to be an ambassador.'' After a slight pause, he added this qualifier, 'to an English speaking country.'' If I had struck any kind of deal with him, I would have broken the law. I told the gentleman that I could not make any promises whatsoever, particularly for ambassadorships to English speaking countries, and under the circumstances I would not be able to do any business with him and I left empty handed.

I nearly always had an aide by my side when I met with any big contributor. I tried to avoid meeting alone with big givers, particularly those I did not know well. An aide could not only take copious and careful notes on the meeting to remind me later important details about the donor and his gift, but could also testify that I flat out refused to agree to any quid pro quo in return for money. If a major donor asked to meet me privately, a red light blinked on because I immediately suspected he wanted to talk about

THE FIRST LESSONS

something inappropriate. I also later learned that this type of person might also be wearing a wire for law enforcement under his suit jacket. My southern gentleman who wanted to be ambassador to an English speaking country subsequently sent the campaign a check for $10,000. I guess good government was worth the ten grand to him.

No president is going to name his enemies to high ranking positions in his administration. He will name like minded people and supporters to the positions he can fill with political appointees. To me, this is the legitimate spoils of war. Those who share his views and philosophy will help implement his policies. It is the beneficial and positive side of patronage. No President can run the government by himself; he needs a team of trusted supporters and advisers. Many prominent American businesspeople who either raised money or gave large sums to candidates have become ambassadors. But I believe this is beneficial to the U.S. government as well as the countries where these people serve. I was named U.S. Consul to Bermuda by President Bill Clinton, for example. I loved the job and I like to think I did a pretty good job for our country as well as the wonderful Bermudians who became my friends.

Patricia Harriman, one of the most famous Georgetown doyennes of her day, was named ambassador to France by Bill Clinton. She served with distinction. The French loved her great style and her political savvy was beneficial to both countries. Elizabeth Frawley Bagley, another amazing Georgetown hostess who opened her spectacular home for many successful fundraisers, became ambassador to Portugal. Elizabeth is also a lawyer with expertise in trade and international relations so she brought substance the job as well as political skill.

Elizabeth was married to Smith Bagley, an heir to the Reynolds tobacco fortune. Smith was a very tall man at 6 feet 4 inches and an extremely gracious gentleman. Sadly, Smith died from complications related to a stroke early in 2010. When Elizabeth was named ambassador to Portugal, she went to ambassador training school, a special tutorial run by the State Department for all appointees. He was asked to attend the school run for ambassador spouses and he did. He always insisted with his tongue firmly in cheek that ambassador spouse school taught him how to do flower arranging and calligraphy for invitations.

A political ambassador has access to the President of the United States that no career diplomat usually has. Some career diplomats who serve in highly sensitive spots obviously are in touch with the White House on a regular basis. But most Foreign Service officers cannot just pick up the phone and dial 202 456 1414, the White House switchboard, and expect to get the President's ear. Longtime friends and supporters can do that and that access can be a win-win for both sides. Political appointees are often better attuned to political conditions as well.

When I was the American Consul to Bermuda, I escorted the Bermuda premier into the White House to meet President Clinton. I could do that because of my relationship with the

THE FIRST LESSONS

President. It was not a session that amounted to anything more than a courtesy call but the Bermuda Premier was thrilled and the visit generated good will.

I am most proud of the work I did for politicians who genuinely cared more about the public interest than their own political interests. They are men and women with a true moral compass. Two of them are the late Senator Edward M. ``Ted'' Kennedy and former Governor Michael S. Dukakis, both sons of Massachusetts and two better people you will never meet in life.

Teddy understood money. His father was a very successful businessman and Ted grew up in a privileged environment. But he could care less about it. I suppose some might say he was rich so he did not know what the alternative was like. But they would be wrong. Ted Kennedy had an instinct and understanding of poverty and need that was uncanny. His empathy was incredible. He was always the first person to pick up a telephone when someone was hurt, sick or died. He wrote personal notes, probably tens of thousands of them over his lifetime that were kind, thoughtful and treasured by the recipients. I have a few of those notes. He always did the right thing. I was proud to know him and support him.

I have often felt lucky to have been drawn into the orbit of Mike Dukakis as early as I was in my fundraising career. I know it kept me out of trouble because Dukakis is the single most pristine person I have ever known. He is totally honest. His standards are clear and high and being his friend and supporter means following the rules as carefully as he does. Michael paid a big political price for his refusal to play the political game as expected when he lost his first gubernatorial reelection campaign to Edward J. King in 1978. He came back and beat King four years later but he never compromised his values or his standards.

Even high minded politicians are not oblivious to their need for campaign money. Without money, they cannot hire staff, rent a campaign headquarters, lease a campaign plane or buy campaign ads and air time. There is no campaign without money. Every candidate recognizes the practical need for raising funds. But there is a right way and a wrong way to raise money.

As my new career as a fundraiser blossomed, I was asked to speak to candidates for the U.S. Senate and House of Representatives and advise them on how to raise sufficient funds for their campaigns.

I developed a set of talking points for them.

I would first tell them that the Internet was a great vehicle for raising money in the 21st century but they could not count on the Internet to get them started. Howard Dean, the former governor of Vermont, was the first presidential candidate to effectively harness the power of the Internet for fundraising. Four years later, Senator Barack Obama mastered the Dean lessons and took Internet fundraising even further raising millions of dollars from small contributors to finance much of his campaign. But before a candidate is well known enough

THE FIRST LESSONS

to tap into that audience, every candidate first needs to raise some ``seed money" to be viewed as credible by the political establishment and the press. A candidate for the U.S. House candidate needs at least $50,000 to $100,000 and a Senate candidate needs between $500,000 and $1 million depending upon the state. In large populous states where television is essential and expensive, such as California and New York, the amount of seed money is even greater. A credible presidential candidate needs to bank about $2.5 to $3 million in seed money to get a campaign off the ground No one will take a candidate seriously unless the candidate's campaign treasury has a decent bank balance.

When I counsel candidates for federal office, I ask them about their past fundraising experiences. Most candidates for the House or Senate have already established themselves by running successfully for mayor, governor, lieutenant governor, state representative or the state senate. Someone helped finance those campaigns. I ask them a series of questions: How did you raise your money in the past? Who donated money to your past campaigns? The beginning of a successful fundraising campaign lies in the candidates' previous givers and existing social networks.

I then tell them that before they hire a campaign manager or retain an outside media consultant, they need to draw up a comprehensive list of every single person they know--every friend, every relative and every business acquaintance with the means to contribute to the campaign or who can approach others to contribute.

◄ THE MONEY GUY

Those personal connections are crucial. I often tell them this story. One day while Mike Dukakis and I were in a car on our way to a fundraiser we were talking about raising money.

"Mike," I said, "Why do you think people give you money?"

He thought for a second before he replied, "Because they like me?"

"With all respect," I said, ``I don't think that's the reason".

"Because they like my issues?" he asked.

"That's not the reason either."

Looking rather exasperated he tried again, "Because they're trying to get influence?"

"No," I said, `` that's not the reason either."

"Well," he said, "I don't need a damn primer on fundraising but why do you think they give me money?"

I said, ``It's very simple. They don't want to say "no" to the person who asked them."

One time during John Kerry's presidential campaign in 2004, a big fundraiser from Hollywood named Skip Paul, a truly wonderful man, flew to Florida to work for six weeks on the campaign. He called his nephew who lived in

Orlando. His nephew was such an ardent Republican he named his dog "W" after President George W. Bush.

He told his nephew, "I want you to know that I am spending six weeks here in Florida working for John Kerry. I put you through college and graduate school and helped you with a down payment on your first house. It would really mean a great deal to me if you would vote for John Kerry on Election Day."

The nephew readily agreed to vote for Kerry but he said, "Uncle Skip, one thing you should know ... you are my only rich relative."

One other time, Senator John Kerry called me and asked me to host a fundraiser at my home in Miami to help him retire debt from a previous campaign. At first, I turned him down. I told him, "John, my friends are all Republicans and I have no economic influence over them. I just can't do it." But he insisted and I finally relented. I called Don Shula, the famed football coach who is a Republican. I invited him to the event but Don protested he did not like Kerry and disagreed with his positions on the issues. Then I reminded him, "But you do like Bob Farmer." When Kerry went through the checks after the event, he came across the $500 from Don Shula and said, "I didn't realize Don Shula liked me so much."

Just think about your own giving, charitable or political. At tax time, when you add up the dollars you gave away in the past year remember who did the asking. The fact of the matter is if you look at your checkbook and look at your contributions, you'll realize that virtually every time you gave was because someone you cared about or was important to you asked. That's why the campaign finance committee is so important.

Many years ago a Republican who was head of a major money management fund in Boston called me and offered to raise money for Michael Dukakis, a Democrat. He was very pleased with some position Dukakis took on an issue of interest to him. I can no longer remember exactly what the issue was but it doesn't matter. What matters is he admired Michael's resolve and commitment. Although he was a Republican and his friends and partners and senior employees at his firm were more likely Republicans than Democrats, they all ponied up money for Mike Dukakis because they did not want to say no to him.

Then I tell candidates that they need to develop a pitch. No salesperson would think of trying to make a sale of anything without ``the pitch''. A candidacy must be sold just like anything else. A candidate needs to tailor his pitch to the audience. A fundraising pitch is different from a pitch to a potential voter the candidate may come across while campaigning. In both cases, however, the pitch needs to be short, succinct and effective. This is my basic pitch for candidates to campaign contributors.

"You've been a friend for many years and I consider you a member of my political family. I am about to embark on the biggest race of my life and I would value your help.

THE FIRST LESSONS ►

I need your support to be successful. Obviously I'd like you to write a check for the maximum amount you can afford (these days that is $2300 for a federal race). *But much more than that, I need your leadership as a member of my finance committee. We'll be having regular meetings to up-date you on the race and you'll be hearing from my pollsters and media advisors as well as my top campaign staff* (usually the campaign manager and the finance director)."

"*The requests I am making of the finance committee members are two-fold. First, I want you to hold a fund-raiser at your home. Second, I need your help to introduce me to some of your friends and acquaintances who have the capacity to join our finance committee.*"

The next part of the pitch explains how and why the candidate will win. In this discussion the candidate needs to make a political case and explain that he or she presently represents as an office holder a certain percentage of the district or state so is already known to a certain percentage of the electorate. The candidate needs to show confidence and predict some significant endorsements. Next the candidate explains the weakness of the opposition and explains how the opponent cannot possibly win. And then the candidate tells with certainty that he or she will have the resources to compete until the end. This is very important. The ability to make a compelling case as to the inevitability of a victory is crucial. Otherwise, friends may write a check but they won't go out and ask their friends to write a check and become actively involved. No one wants to go out on a limb for a lost cause.

These days it is crucial to develop a web site. A web site is increasingly the public face of a campaign. More and more people use computers and rely upon the Internet to conduct research on everything from household appliances to political candidates. The web site must put the best foot forward for the campaign because it will not only showcase the candidate's positions on the issues but will also be the base for recruiting volunteers and soliciting donations. There are a lot of web site developers and designers but a good way to begin is to look at the web sites of other successful campaigns and adopt and adapt the best points.

I discourage candidates from using their life savings to run for public office. Most candidates with a track record of public service are not independently wealthy. There are exceptions but most career politicians have modest means because they spent their most lucrative earning years on a public payroll. No political job pays nearly as much as a private sector job. Gambling the house money or the retirement fund and financial security of a family is simply insane for anyone. I tell candidates that if you are unable to raise sufficient funds, that is an indication that you may be over-reaching in terms of your ambition. I caution them that at the end of the campaign your campaign manager will come to you and say that if we just had an additional $50,000 or $100,000 we could increase our media buy and that would be the difference between winning and losing.

THE FIRST LESSONS

At this point it is very enticing to go out and mortgage the family home because ego is on the line. I tell candidates to resist that temptation. Don't do it. When you have lost the campaign, you will be out of work and you will be labeled a loser. The fair weather friends will disappear. You will be left with your family. To put your family at a financial disadvantage for ambition is just wrong. Candidates can get into a financial hole that hobbles them for years.

The other thing I advise candidates to do is be consistent on fundamental moral issues. I'm not an issues guy but one thing I've learned along the way is that you don't change your position on moral issues such as a woman's right to choose, gay rights or other basic issues. You can make arguments for and against taxes at different times in response to different conditions. But moral issues like the death penalty or choice are fundamental character issues. I say to the candidate that I'm not going to tell you what position to take.... that's up to you.... but don't change for political expediency. Changing a position on a fundamental issue makes voters understandably wary. If a candidate can change on a profound moral question such as choice or a human rights issue, it suggests the candidate cannot be trusted on any issue. I have always been a closet admirer of Mitt Romney, the former governor of Massachusetts, because of his great business success. I suspect one reason his presidential campaign did so badly in 2008 was because he flip flopped on major issues. He took a progressive stance on gay rights and abortion when running against Ted Kennedy for the Senate in 1994 and

THE MONEY GUY

when running for governor of Massachusetts but took the opposite position to run for President as a Republican. Voters see right through that type of posturing.

For every campaign for the House or Senate, there is a history and lists of contributors to past campaigns for that office. These are obvious targets of opportunity. But, one word of caution: These folks may have given in the past, not out of conviction, but because they didn't want to say "no" to the person who asked them. So they may or may not be prime prospects for another Democrat or Republican seeking the same position. Of course, you know they have enough money to write a check and having given once, a person is more likely to give again. Political giving is an acquired habit just like any other.

In every district or state there are a number of "bundlers". These are people with a track record of success in raising money through their own network of friends and business associates. I suggest that candidates identify these "bundlers" and then request a meeting with them. A phone call is a short cut but if a person agrees to take a meeting, the candidate has a much better chance of making a case and closing the deal in person. I tell candidates to identify friends of the bundlers. A mutual friend can call in advance and urge the bundler to meet with you and say something like "I think it would serve you well to meet with Joe because Joe is going to win this race and it's important that someone as prominent as you have a relationship with the next Congressman or Senator."

THE FIRST LESSONS

I give candidates a script for meeting with the bundler. This is what they need to say:

"I know of you by your excellent reputation, but I'd appreciate it if you'd give me a two minute bio of where you're from, where you went to school , tell me about your family and finally tell me how you've been so successful."

These two minute bios always last a lot longer than two minutes. People really like talking about themselves and about their success. Politicians are particularly enamored with the sound of their own voices. Most politicians need to make certain you know they are the smartest people in the room. The exception to this is former House Majority Leader Dick Gephardt of Missouri. Among politicians, Dick was the best listener I ever met. He leans in and seems to drink in the person who is talking and shows genuine interest. It is a real talent and I'm sure it contributed to his success as a political leader and as a fundraiser.

Giving a potential contributor the chance to talk about himself matters. It is astonishing how many things a candidate will find in common with a potential contributor. There are common experiences, common schools, common friends or they may serve on the same corporate or non-profit or charitable board as another close friend. These commonalities can nurture and strengthen an embryonic friendship. These meetings have a dual agenda. The candidate needs to convince the bundler that he or she will win and it is in their interest to begin a professional and personal relationship with him. The bundler also has an agenda. Most

THE MONEY GUY

bundlers are men, but some are women. The bundler wants to educate the candidate, be appreciated and be a person of wisdom and expertise that the successful candidate will call upon when he takes office.

One time during Michael Dukakis' presidential campaign in 1988, I was meeting at the Waldorf Towers in New York City with a gentleman whom I hoped would contribute $100,000 to the Democratic National Committee, the maximum amount allowed under the law. He knew exactly what I was after and I knew he knew. But I made the standard pitch and he reached into his pocket and pulled out a check that had been written and signed.

He placed it on the table in between us and said, ``Mr. Farmer, may I ask one question?" I didn't want to appear too anxious but I did keep my eye on the check. "Go ahead" I said.

He then asked the best question I've ever heard in political fundraising. "Mr. Farmer, is this hello or goodbye?"

He was asking if this was the beginning or the end of our relationship. I, of course, said that it was the beginning but it taught me a very important lesson. If a campaign is successful, people want to know that you will remain their friend, remember their generosity and return their phone calls. Follow up is important.

I tell candidates that a great percentage of time, more time than they realize, will be spent raising money, one on one,

THE FIRST LESSONS

on the phone and in breakfasts, lunches and dinners in addition to attending fundraisers. Moreover, the beginning of the campaign will require a major investment of time into fundraising because by the end, the candidate needs to be doing straight campaign and political events to rally the voters and get them to the polls and there will be no time for fundraising. The arc of a campaign is always the same: the major fundraising push comes at the beginning and the biggest expenditures come at the end.

Finally, I talk to candidates about the importance of finance committees. I often get asked to serve on committees and boards of all sorts. When I am asked to serve my first question is: ``What is this going to cost me?'' My second question is:``Who else is on the board?'' A board is another social network opportunity. The candidate needs to create a sense of fellowship and shared cause among the finance committee members. This band of brothers and sisters will be more effective if they feel some camaraderie and friendships with the other members. One way of doing that is to ask each member to introduce him or herself and to describe what he or she does for a living at the first few meetings. People want to know other successful people and to create relationships with them. The more prestigious folks you can get to serve on your committee and attend meetings the more this will attract other successful people.

When I was treasurer of the Democratic Governor's Association, I was invited by Governor Booth Gardner

THE MONEY GUY

of Washington State to visit him and talk about fundraising. He was an heir to the Weyerhaeuser fortune and used much of his own money for his first campaign. When he ran for re-election, his wife thought he ought to diversify the funding sources.

We had dinner on the top floor of a big building in Seattle with a gorgeous view of the mountains. We had drinks and chatted for several hours.

About six months later I saw Booth and asked him how the campaign was going? "Great" he replied. "I remember one thing from the dinner we had". While I was a little bit disappointed that he remembered only one thing because we had talked for hours, I asked him what it was.

"Before we had dinner, if I had an event at someone's home in Tacoma, and walked in and it was a large crowd, I'd say to myself, Gee, I didn't realize how popular I was in Tacoma. After our dinner I'd say to myself, Gee, I didn't realize how popular my host was in Tacoma."

Of course, there are limits on how popular one is. I often tell this story to potential candidates.

I always got a big kick out of seeing my name in the newspaper and seeing myself on television talking about politics or standing by the candidate.

One day I was sitting in a campaign senior staff meeting and one of my aides came to the door and said, ``Mr.

THE FIRST LESSONS

Farmer, the New York Times is on the phone."

I puffed out my chest and announced, "I'll have to take it."

I took the phone and a voice asked, "Is this Robert Farmer?"

"Yes," I replied.

"Would you consider a sixty day trial subscription to the New York Times?"

Well, that took me down a few notches!

When I first became involved in the Anderson campaign, I admit I was quite naïve and innocent. But I learned fast and I quickly became caught up and enamored with the process and playing a leadership role in political campaigns and establishing connections between the candidates and contributors. In short, I loved the game. Despite the occasional craven politician and despite the excesses, I kept at it for 30 long years and still cannot resist a call for help from a friend. Someone once asked me why I still do it. I responded with a line from my friend, J. Joseph Grandmaison, the gifted New Hampshire political operative and longtime member of the Export-Import Board. I said, ``because it is a fleeting moment of almost being relevant."

CHAPTER **3**

Only in America

I was born on September 23, 1938 in Cleveland, Ohio, the middle son in a family of three boys. My mother used to say, ``Sterling is the oldest and the good looking one and Brent is the youngest and the smart one." People would notice she had not mentioned the third son and ask, `` What about Bob?" Mother always said, ``Oh ...Bob is the rich one". Our parents saw to it that all three of us had the opportunity to do well but the story always made me laugh.

I consider myself a fairly average and typical person and I believe that is why I get along with people so easily. I grew up in Ohio at a time when the state was prosperous and thriving. Ohio developed a strong industrial and manufacturing base in the late 19th century because of its great rivers and proximity to the Great Lakes. The state's many factories generated thousands of jobs and produced auto parts, coal, iron ore, steel and petroleum products.

Our parents' wedding was a great social event in Akron, Ohio, the hometown of my mother, Eleanor Sandberg Farmer in 1933. The headline on article on my parent's wedding in the Akron Beacon Journal society page story read: ``Sandberg-Farmer Ceremony among Largest Nuptial Events of Season". The Journal ran a photograph at the top of the page showing my mother in her white satin wedding gown with her two sisters who were her attendants. The story said they wore aquamarine blue taffeta. A huge bouquet of white orchids and lilies of the valley filled Mother's arms. According to the article, 100 wedding guests attended a reception at the home of mother's parents. Flowers from grandmother's garden decorated the house for the September wedding. The newlyweds went to Georgian Bay on Lake Huron in Canada for a two week honeymoon.

The Great Depression still oppressed the country. Franklin Delano Roosevelt had won election in November of 1932 and the New Deal programs designed to ease the suffering caused by the collapse of the stock market in 1929 and the subsequent collapse of the economy were just being introduced. There was no sign of the depression in the Akron Beacon Journal society page story, however. Our father subsequently lost his job at the India Tire and Rubber Company in Akron when the company collapsed during the Depression but he then went to work at Sand Products Company where my grandfather held the position of treasurer. Our grandparents worked hard to make life better for their children and our parents did the same thing for us.

THE MONEY GUY

Our parents' fathers were self-made men who started with nothing and became very successful. My mother's father, Axel Sandberg, was born in Houtzdale, Pennsylvania in 1882. He began working in a coal mine when he was 12 years old. He met John A. Adolf at an ice cream social. Adolf later because the president of the coal company. My grandfather was an ambitious man and wanted to set up his own business. Adolf helped him establish a general store in 1903. He sold the store in 1914 and operated a coal mine for a couple of years before moving to Akron and setting up the Waldorf Ice Cream Company, a very successful ice cream manufacturing concern. We always called him by his first name, Axel. Axel was a bit of a wild man. He was a real self-made man's man who loved to play poker. My poor grandmother got pregnant nearly every time they engaged in marital relations. She had six children and five survived. After the sixth, she shut him off. She had enough children. So he always kept a girlfriend on the side. One year, he and my father were driving to Florida. They stopped at a hotel in a small southern town that turned out to be a whore house. Axel was delighted. My father, his son in law, was a very proper Victorian gentleman and he was totally horrified. The different reactions tell you something about both men. Axel never went to college but he sent all five of his surviving children to college, including the girls. My mother graduated from Wheaton College in Norton, Massachusetts. It was highly unusual in those years for a young woman from Akron to go east to college.

My father's father, August Farmer, had an even more amazing

story. We called him Granddaddy. He always said he was born in the foothills of the Carpathian Mountains. He was never quite sure of which country it was because he said the boundaries were always changing. An educated guess is he was from somewhere in the Austria-Hungary area. As my brother Sterling recalls the family tale, a number of families from my father's home town chartered a boat to travel to America. My father was about 9 or 10 years old at the time. Some married men, including his father, planned to travel alone and promised to send later for the rest of their families. My Granddaddy August was very sharp for a young boy and he figured out right away that his father had no intention of sending for the family. Evidently my great grandfather was not very responsible.

So Granddaddy tagged along and mingled with other kids boat side and everyone figured he belonged to one of the other families. He hid below deck until he got violently seasick. When he went up for air, he came face to face with his father. He always told us that they both turned abruptly away from one another and walked away without saying a word proving that Granddaddy had my great-grandfather's number exactly right.

When the ship arrived in New York, he snuck away and somehow eluded customs and Ellis Island. He lived on the streets of the city. Sterling says he told him that he claimed he learned English that way but in fact, it was a mixture of Italian, Yiddish, and English with a lot of swear words. August lived on the street for about a year. He dug food out of garbage cans and begged, borrowed and stole to survive. He was shining the shoes of a man one day who asked him about his family. Granddaddy told him he had none so the man offered him a spot in his orphanage. At that time in the late 19th century, foundling homes in New York City cared for orphans and then sent them to the Midwest to farm families for adoption. A warm bed, three meals a day and a chance at being adopted by a farm family sounded like a good deal to August so he moved into the orphanage.

A supporter of the orphanage, Graham Sterling, paid for my grandfather's passage from New York to Minnesota. Sterling remembers this story well because he and our father were named after this man. Mr. Sterling had been very generous to the orphanage and was approached again by the orphanage administrators for a donation but he resisted because he had given a great deal of money in the past. But just then, Mr. Sterling's young son came into the room with his piggy bank and asked if he could help the children. The boy had recently recovered from a serious illness and his generosity so moved his father that Mr. Sterling immediately agreed to sponsor one more boy. That boy was my grandfather, a little red head who was adopted by a Minnesota farm family.

Granddaddy was adopted by a wonderful family whose last name was Farmer so he took the name of his adopted family. His actual last name was Neustadt which means new city or new state in German. Neustadt was my father's and brother Sterling's middle name. Sterling was always told the N stands for Nothing because our grandmother thought it sounded "foreign" and didn't care to be reminded of it. Granddaddy August went on to become a pioneer educator and consultant and a successful businessman. He graduated from Carleton College at the age of 27 in 1899 and then studied law at the University of Minnesota. He was a teacher, principal and superintendent of schools in St. Cloud, Minnesota and Evanston, Illinois.

My grandfather was a very bright and talented man. He directed a study of Wisconsin normal schools and helped do a study of New York City schools. He was a wonderful teacher. He taught me mathematics at the dining room table when I was having difficulty with math and he tutored Sterling in algebra as well. Sterling says that our grandfather used his own money to quietly educate children he felt deserved a higher education. He also studied food problems during World War I and conducted a survey on state government for the state of Michigan.

Then in mid-life he switched careers. A close friend got very sick and my grandmother nursed him back to health. When the friend recovered, he formed the Sand Products Corporation in Cleveland and invited my grandfather to join it as an investor and partner. The company mined sand in the upper Great Lakes and then delivered it to foundries for use in the manufacturing process. Granddaddy joined the firm as treasurer and remained with the firm until his death. Granddaddy invested a great deal of money into it though my grandmother would not let him invest the family farm in Illinois. She wanted to be sure she had a roof over her head if things did not work out. Things worked out better than he could have anticipated. He received dividends of $35,000 a year from that investment during the Great Depression which was extraordinary given the time. He set up a Trust Fund for every grandchild and the revenue from those funds paid for our summer camps, bought braces for our teeth and for college and graduate school tuition. It was a remarkable legacy for a little boy who stowed away on a ship to come to America.

August Farmer married Nellie Rafferty in 1899. Our grandmother Nell could trace her heritage directly right back to Captain Increase Child who fought in the American Revolutionary War under Major General Philip Schuyler who was head of the Northern Army of the Revolution. Increase Child was born in Woodstock, Connecticut in 1740 and died there 50 years later. His daughter Olin, named after her mother, is our link to America's War for Independence. Our father applied for membership in the Children of the American Revolution when he was a boy and was accepted. We keep copies of his application in our family records.

Among the family papers that survive, I have a copy of a letter my grandfather August wrote to my father on his 46th birthday on February 14, 1948. I would have been nine years old at the time and we were living in a home in Lakewood, then one of the biggest suburbs of Cleveland. My grandfather wrote from his winter home in Miami

Beach, Florida. ``I remember very distinctly the day you were born,'' he wrote. ``The teachers and pupils knew of the event and I believe that on that day you received no less than 1000 valentines each one designed by a pupil of the Seward School in Minneapolis.'' In 1902, grandfather was still working as an educator.

It was a lovely and loving letter. He praised my father for having worked so hard to achieve success in his job.

``You have had to work, struggle and fight for whatever you have achieved,'' grandfather wrote in his perfect penmanship. ``It has not been easy but of greatest benefit since it is the struggle, continuous and persistent that develops in the individual the inherent peculiarities -- his personality, character and capacities.''

When Granddaddy died at the age of 84 in June 1956, Dr. Peter H. Samsom, a minister at the West Shore Unitarian Church in Cleveland, spoke eloquently about August N. Farmer at his memorial service.

I was struck by Dr. Samsom's description of Granddaddy's views of religion. Granddaddy was not much of a church goer.

He said, ``His was a questioning and seeking mind, ever reaching out for greater truth, surer knowledge, better ways of living and working together. With profound respect for the spirit and findings of science, he developed for himself an intelligent faith in the creative universal force of

◄ THE MONEY GUY

life, which he personally felt was worthy of reverence. In matters of religion, he once advised a grandson to `ask questions but avoid arguments' and always to maintain respect for the faith of another. Every man ultimately alone must reach his own conclusions about life, he believed. None can do your thinking for you. So he advised, be honest with yourself, and do all you can to make the most of your own potential."

Dr. Samsom also said: ``In his teaching and writing, his school administration and his public service; in his research work, his conservation work in wartime, in exploring ways to put city government on a sound business basis, in advancing more progressive ways of teaching, and in his fresh approach to educating for modern salesmanship and his seeking out new possibilities for industrial development – to name but a few areas of his labors – August Farmer was always breaking new ground and planting new seeds which were to bear rich fruit in the lives of many besides himself.

``He never forgot his own beginnings, difficult and struggling," the minister said. ``His gratitude for whatever blessings that became his sparked his devotion to work on behalf of orphans conducted by the Brotherhood of American Yeomen; and that gratitude spoke through many a helping hand he extended to needy students, never forgetting that he was once one himself."

I was fortunate that I did not have to struggle because my parents and grandparents smoothed the way for me and

ONLY IN AMERICA

for my brothers. Our parents were strict but loving. They required us to do chores but they provided us with a wonderful home and every opportunity to succeed.

Lakewood, Ohio was a booming suburb just ten minutes from downtown Cleveland in our childhood. Our home was in the more affluent section, across the street from Lake Erie and a 65 or 70 foot cliff that dropped straight down to the water. My brother Brent once counted the number of elementary school children in our neighborhood. There were 56.

In that more innocent, safer time, it was expected that a first grade boy would walk by himself the half mile to the Lincoln School, our local public elementary school. We walked home for lunch and then back again for afternoon classes. Mother did not work outside the home. We were fortunate to have her steady presence at home.

I was very close to my mother, perhaps closer than my brothers. When we grew up, my brothers had their own families but as a gay man, my parents were my family. So I spoke to my mother virtually every day. She was a delightful conversationalist. She was bright, well educated and interested in everything. She loved to gossip but I cannot recall her ever saying a negative nasty word about anyone. My father was much the same way. Once when I was at Dartmouth, Mother had clipped for me some photographs and stories from the Cleveland Plain Dealer about people we knew. When she asked me about one of the photographs, of a woman the family knew well, I said I could not remember receiving that picture. It turned out that my father did not send it along because it was an unattractive photo of the woman. He was a consummate gentleman and quite scrupulous. Mother always said that Dad slept in the nude but when he put his trousers on in the morning, he would turn his back to her as he zipped up the fly. As the oldest of five children, Mother held the extended family together after our grandparents died.

We grew up in a comfortable home. Our grandfathers had made sure their children, our parents, were educated. My father, Sterling N. Farmer Sr., graduated from Drake University and then attended Harvard Business School. He was working in Akron when he met my mother.

My father was 36 when I was born. At that time, he was considered an older father. My mother always said that an older father would not play baseball with me but he would play golf at the country club. He was not a pal the way sons are pals with their Dads these days. But I learned golf at an early age by accompanying him to the country club. He was a smart man, a good provider and a very good role model.

Our childhoods took place during World War II when Cleveland prospered because so many products needed to fight the war were manufactured in the area.

I was often an indifferent student. Education was simply not a priority for me so one summer my parents sent me off to board at Culver Military Academy in Indiana, a prep school that used the military model, to see if Culver could shape me up. The biggest discovery I made at Culver had nothing to do with academics. When I was 12 years old, I realized I was gay.

When horsing around with my classmates in the seventh grade, I realized I was sexually attracted to other boys. I knew it was not ``normal'' yet I did not feel guilty about it. At the same time, I instinctively realized that these feelings had to be kept a secret from everyone. From youth, I had a very strong sense of self-preservation.

When I was a boy, gay men were called ``queers'' and ``faggots''. *Every* state had laws on the books making consensual sexual activity between people of the same sex a crime. My home state of Ohio did not repeal its sodomy criminal laws until 1974. In 1950, the year I realized I was gay, 91 gay State Department employees were fired for being ``security risks'' ostensibly because their sexuality made them subject to blackmail. During the McCarthy era, it was as dangerous to be gay as to be a member of the Communist Party.

No intelligent boy would want to known as gay so I grew up wishing I was heterosexual and telling no one, not my parents, my brothers, my friends, of my true nature. I actually got married to a wonderful woman when I was 30 years old. I tried to convince myself that the feelings for men were a phase that I would outgrow. After five years of marriage to a woman I truly did love but with whom I was fundamentally incompatible, I sought a divorce in 1973. I

◄ THE MONEY GUY

never told her the real reason until much later. Fortunately, she later met and married a good man and had a long happy marriage. But I did come to terms with myself. I was not getting any younger and I faced up to the importance of being true to myself as Granddaddy had always advised.

My personal realization coincided with the dawning of the gay rights era. In 1969, New York City police raided a gay bar, the Stonewall Inn in Greenwich Village triggering spontaneous violent demonstrations by gay men and lesbians who were fed up with being oppressed. The first Gay Liberation Day parade took place in New York the following year. And I met Tim McNeill in 1975 who became my partner for the next 17 years.

Tim was 11 years younger than I and he had no intention of being furtive or hidden away about his sexuality and our relationship. This had a big impact on my life. Tim's uncle, his father's brother, was a renowned and learned Jesuit priest, Fr. John J. McNeill. His uncle wrote a bestselling book, The Church and the Homosexual, in 1975. Fr. McNeill was a psychotherapist and scholar who argued in the book that gay men and lesbians were part of God's plan. Through careful scholarship, he showed that the Bible could be interpreted in different ways and challenged the traditional conservative assumption that homosexuality was a grave sin. His book hit the best seller list but a year after its publication; he received an order from the highest levels of the Vatican, the Congregation for the Doctrine of the Faith under Cardinal Ratzinger, now Pope Benedict XVI, ordering him to not engage in any further public comment on the book. He agreed and kept silent for the next nine years while continuing his ministry to gays and lesbians. Then in 1988, the Cardinal ordered him to give up all ministry to gay people including psychotherapy. He refused as a matter of conscience and was expelled from the Society of Jesus after nearly 40 years as a Jesuit priest.

Fr. McNeill took vows of celibacy as a priest and was faithful to those vows but he acknowledged he was gay in a national interview with Tom Brokaw on NBC's Today Show during his book tour. Fr. McNeill had a remarkable life. He was taken prisoner by the Germans during military service during World War II and survived that ordeal. He now lives in Florida with his partner and continues to blog and minister to gay men and lesbians.

So Tim influenced me to be more open about my sexuality. But I was also a risk taker and always felt that I was entitled to live my life as I wanted to live it. My Granddaddy August had always said be true to yourself. I had never been shy. I was always an extrovert. My brother Sterling tells the story of when I was 5 years old and he was 9, we had a dental appointment. Our mother dropped us off at the front door of the building and went to park the car. I remembered where the office was and grabbed Sterling's hand and led him up three flights of stairs to the dentist. I walked in ahead of him and announced, "I'm Bob Farmer and this is my brother and we are here for a dental appointment." I was only five and I was already the assertive one.

THE MONEY GUY

My entrepreneurial instinct became apparent in my childhood. I started a school newspaper, *The Lincoln Log,* at my elementary school and I launched a band when I was in junior high school. This was a time before rock and roll and we actually had to play real music.

I also seemed to have a knack for being in the right place at the right time. I took a train to Dartmouth to begin college and met George Gund, the CEO of the biggest bank in Cleveland, who was taking his daughter to college. I talked to him because I had known his son from high school and asked him if I could get a summer job at the Cleveland Trust company. He very kindly gave me a job at the bank for four summers, the first two as a bank teller. Then I worked as an intern in the real estate loan department. One of my jobs was to separate all the checks that came in each day into piles: one for checks written on the main office of Cleveland Trust; the second for checks written from other branches; the third for other banks in the city; and the fourth for out of town banks. I noticed that a lot of people with real estate loans at the Cleveland Trust had other accounts at other banks. I suggested we draft a letter to them and encourage them to consolidate their banking at Cleveland Trust where they could expect preferential treatment because they were existing customers. Mr. Gund was impressed by that initiative and when I applied to Harvard, he wrote a letter of recommendation for me. The recommendation helped a lot because he was not only a graduate of Harvard and Harvard Business School but he served on Harvard's prestigious Board of Overseers for six years.

I was always willing to take chances. When we were children, we dropped a rope from the attic window of our house and swung from the window to the ground. A neighbor and mother of one of my chums, was asked whether she worried about her son engaging in such a dangerous activity. She said, ``Oh no... I knew Bob would go first."

My brother Brent remembers that I borrowed Sterling's snow skis when I was an undergraduate at Dartmouth. Even though I could not ski at all, I aggressively went off the ski jump in New Hampshire. He remembers this story because I broke Sterling's skis but he views it as an early indication of my willingness to take a great leap into the unknown, a predilection that proved to be helpful in my business career.

I also liked people and enjoyed meeting new people but I was always very guarded because I was gay. I read *The Best Little Boy in the World*, a memoir of growing up gay, when it was first published in 1973. The book has been continuously printed since then and is considered a classic. The book was published under the pseudonym John Reid.

John Reid is really Andrew Tobias, the noted financial writer who later became treasurer of the Democratic National Committee, a position I also held. Andrew is frequently described as the first gay treasurer of the DNC. In fact, he was the first treasurer who was known to be gay because I had the job before he did.

Andrew is nine years younger than I am but he had similar

THE MONEY GUY

experiences growing up. I completely identified with him. He kept his sexual preference private and did not come out until he was 23 in 1970. Though he was younger than I, we came out within a few years of one another because societal attitudes towards gay men were beginning to shift.

It is painful for me to recollect my boyhood and those early adult years as a closeted gay man. I was desperately lonely and I always felt like an outsider looking in. When I was at Dartmouth, I sought out the services of a psychiatrist because I was also profoundly depressed at the time. Yet I could not even bring myself to tell the doctor the true reason for my misery. I was afraid it would somehow be noted on my school record and haunt me for the rest of my life.

The situation improved when I enrolled in Harvard Law School because there were gay bars in Boston and finally I was able to meet other gay men. I remember spotting another classmate at a gay bar in Boston. I was paralyzed with horror at being seen but he casually walked over to me and made a joke about finding one another in this location. It was a relief to find someone else who was like me.

Yet I was not being open about my sexuality at school. My closest friends at Harvard Law School had no idea I was gay. After my Army service, I met a law school classmate who was gay. We were never involved sexually but we were in the same boat so we shared an off campus apartment. He was two years younger than I and we remained friends long after graduation. Tim and I once visited him and his partner in Beverly Hills. He had inherited a great deal of money and owned a huge mansion that had once belonged to the actor Tony Curtis. A butler served us dinner. I told Tim that I never wanted to live in Beverly Hills. Although there were wealthier people than I in Boston, no one would ever know because of the Boston tradition of never being showy about personal wealth. In Los Angeles, I would never have been able to compete and would have been considered a peon!

I never told my parents I was gay but they eventually knew.

My parents were in Florida one winter visiting an aunt and uncle. They went out to dinner one night and my aunt had too much to drink and apparently was tired of my parents bragging about their brilliant successful children and blurted out, ``Your millionaire son is a fairy.'' Mother was so offended that my parents moved into a motel that night and did not speak to her for several years. But mother called me on the phone afterwards and said she had a personal question for me. I had a feeling of what she was about to ask. She asked, ``Is there anything unusual about your relationship with Tim?'' Tim and I had concocted the fiction for outsiders that we were just ``roommates'' and we actually had set up separate bedrooms in the house in Brookline when we first bought the house.

I could not lie to my mother. So I said, ``Of course.'' She said,``Oh!'' We never really discussed it again. I never thought Mother would have a problem with my sexuality. She was a sophisticated woman, well educated and well read. I later learned that when she repeated the conversation to my father, Dad said, ``I've known that for years,'' but he had never thought it necessary to discuss it with her or me for that matter.

When my parents celebrated their 50th wedding anniversary in 1983, my brothers and I wanted to throw a big party at their local country club in Cleveland so all their friends could attend. Mother, however, said she wanted the family, including all the children and grandchildren, to gather for a private family vacation at the Greenbrier Resort in White Sulphur Springs, West Virginia. Much later, I learned it was because she did not want to risk any embarrassment when I showed up with my then partner Tim. My mother and I were close and I'm quite sure my sexual preference made no difference in her feelings for me but she was a product of her time and I'm certain wanted to spare everyone, including me, any awkwardness at a time of celebration.

If my parents were products of their time, so was I. I was not a Baby Boomer but I benefited from the social and political upheaval of the 1960's and 1970's. The boomers rejected the status quo and demanded and created a more open society. This dramatically improved the environment for gay men and lesbians So much so that as I progressed in my second career as a political fundraiser, my sexual preference never became an issue.

CHAPTER 4

A New Beginning

The Anderson campaign fell short of victory but it introduced me to a whole new world of politics. Politics injected a new element into my life. The campaign gave me a second lease on life in my 40's when I was beginning to wonder if I had done all that I was meant to do. I relished the excitement and thrill of political campaigns.

Political candidates and operatives often talk about the let down they experience after Election Day when the campaign ends and there is nothing left to do. Some campaign operatives actually complain about experiencing something similar to post partum depression. The baby, the election, has been born. The anticipation is over. The 24-hour day seven day a week obsessive focus of the drive to Election Day completely disappears. They feel empty and depressed.

I was not at all depressed, quite the contrary. The experience revved me up. I wanted to stay in the game, learn

◄ THE MONEY GUY

more about this amazing political process and find my next campaign. And it was more than just excitement and the proximity to power. I felt as though I was part of something big, something that mattered. I had never fully appreciated the role of political campaigns in our democracy. Seeing political campaigns from the inside renewed my appreciation for representative democracy. And I truly felt I had something to offer as a fundraiser.

Living in Massachusetts, I was acutely aware of anticipation building for the 1982 gubernatorial campaign. In 1978, Michael S. Dukakis, a Democratic governor who lived not far from me on Perry Street in Brookline, lost the Democratic primary campaign in his bid for reelection to Edward J. King, a conservative Democrat who represented a throwback to a good old boy bygone era in Massachusetts politics. King was a decent enough guy and we actually became social friends many years later in Florida long after he had retired from public life but his campaign adroitly exploited political mistakes made by Dukakis and anticipated the unquestionable conservative resurgence in the United States manifested by Ronald Reagan's presidential victory in 1980 and the approval of an anti-tax referendum in Massachusetts called Proposition 2 1/2. As I noted before, Reagan carried Massachusetts (if barely) in 1980 and Massachusetts is considered one of the most liberal Democratic states in the nation.

Mike Dukakis, sobered by his loss, had been planning a comeback ever since his defeat. The 1982 rematch

A NEW BEGINNING

campaign, a real old fashioned grudge match, was the talk of the political community in the Bay State and I wanted to be a part of it.

I did not know Dukakis personally but I admired his reformer style. When Dukakis won the Democratic gubernatorial primary in 1974, he had beaten state Attorney General Bob Quinn, another decent guy but like Ed King, Quinn represented the old way of doing things. Dukakis represented a new generation type of politician, an independent minded reformer and progressive and voters had high expectations for him when he swept into office in 1974.

I had become very good friends with Josiah ``Si'' Spaulding and his wife Helen during the Anderson campaign. Si Spaulding was a major player in Massachusetts Republican politics. He came from an old established Massachusetts family but earned a reputation as a bit of a maverick. He had been the Republican nominee against Senator Kennedy in 1970 and run unsuccessfully for state Attorney General in 1974. He led an unsuccessful effort at the 1968 Republican National Convention to deny the nomination to Richard M. Nixon and backed New York Governor Nelson A. Rockefeller instead. Si was also a very successful businessman. He was the founder and President of the Massachusetts Spaulding Rehabilitation Hospital in Boston, one of the nation's best hospitals.

In talking to Si about my interest in politics, I said to him, ``Si, you should run for governor.'' He said, ``Bob, I'm not going to run for governor but I will tell you who you should work for, Mike Dukakis."

Even from my essentially non-political perspective, it was clear Dukakis had made political errors rather than substantive ones. Although I was not involved in his administration during the first term, I heard all the stories and many people said he tried to do too much at once and he seemed to forget who his friends were. Over time, I came to appreciate the need for politicians to adopt narrow achievable agendas when they took office. But at the end of 1980, I was less concerned about the past and much more focused on becoming part of his comeback effort. So I called a friend, Richard Zeckhauser, a champion bridge player who was a highly regarded economics professor at the John F. Kennedy School of Government at Harvard. Dukakis had taken a teaching position at the Kennedy School after his defeat and was planning his comeback from there. I asked Dick Zeckhauser to introduce us.

I took the professor and Mike Dukakis to lunch at my country club, Brae Burn, an elegant high end club in nearby West Newton, one of the nicer western suburbs of Boston. I admit I wanted to impress the former governor. Had I known him better, I would not have sprung for a pricey lunch at Brae Burn. I subsequently learned that Mike Dukakis would have been just as happy eating hotdogs by the back of a caterer's truck. Mike is a man of very simple tastes and he does not stand on ceremony of any sort. His usual lunch is a bowl of soup and half a sandwich. This simplicity permeates his life.

A NEW BEGINNING

Michael owned an old-fashioned push reel mower which he used to cut the grass of his tiny lawn in Brookline. Most people didn't even know that lawn mowers came without motors. Years later, I would see him walking by himself at out of state Democratic Governor's Conferences while other governors would strut in surrounded by six burly state cops. They thought the heavy security made them look more important. Michael never traveled with security. He could care less about the perception of power. He believed being accompanied by armed guards made him less safe. He resisted Secret Service protection longer than he should have in the 1988 presidential campaign. He only became persuaded when an overly enthusiastic mob of Greek-Americans in the Astoria neighborhood of Queens nearly took him apart limb by limb. It was a frightening evening for all of us who were there and this near brush with disaster convinced him to accept the inevitable.

For our first meeting, I had prepared my sales pitch. I was honest with the former governor about my burning desire to be involved in politics. I told Dukakis that I had never come as alive as I had in the Anderson campaign. But I also wanted him to recognize that I could bring something to the table and help his campaign. I told him I wanted to be his finance chairman if he ran for reelection as governor and I described my new network of fundraisers from the Anderson campaign who were poised to help him.

Dukakis was very polite and he thanked me but he said he had been in politics for decades and appreciated my offer

◂ **THE MONEY GUY**

but he couldn't name me as a finance chairman because he did not know me well enough.

I respected his view. It was true. He did not know me at all. So I volunteered to host a series of $500 a person lunches at the Harvard Club in downtown Boston and promised that each lunch would include 10 or 12 people and I would demonstrate that I could raise him some serious money in the 12 weeks remaining in the year.

He agreed. I set up eight lunches in November and December of 1980 and invited the people I had met on the Anderson campaign at $500 per person.

Those lunches were revelatory to me. They proved that I picked the right candidate. Dukakis was mesmerizing in his command of public policy. He also remembered every single name which amazed me because I can never remember names. Name tags were invented for people like me. The most effective politicians have that gift for recalling names. At each lunch, the group would stand around, be introduced to Dukakis and have cocktails and then sit down for a light lunch. Dukakis would do his pitch and take questions addressing each person by name. The participants all came from my Anderson network and most of them had never met Mike Dukakis but they were definitely his type. They wanted good government and without exception every one left lunch deeply impressed. So I not only raised some money for the Dukakis gubernatorial campaign but I helped recruit a new network of fundraisers for him.

A NEW BEGINNING

I was struck that everyone still addressed Dukakis as ``governor'' even though he had lost the election. Some years later when I served as US Consul General to Bermuda, I hosted Ted and Vicki Kennedy as well as Don and Mary Anne Shula. When I introduced them to one another in the living room of the residence, Don Shula said, `` Senator, nice to meet you.'' Kennedy replied, ``Coach, it's nice to meet you.'' After the introductions, they called one another ``Ted'' and ``Don'' and I realized that no one is ever offended if you recognize their title.

In late December of 1980, Dukakis invited me to a Christmas party at his house. He wanted me to meet John Sasso. Sasso was a young rising political operative then in his early 30's who ran the campaigns and managed the district office of Rep. Gerry Studds, the Democrat who represented the South Shore of Massachusetts as well as Cape Cod and the Islands in Congress. John had earned national credentials as a field operative for Ted Kennedy in his 1980 presidential campaign. Dukakis had just hired Sasso to run his rematch campaign in 1982 and he wanted Sasso to check me out before agreeing to include me in his campaign.

We both knew the stakes so we gravitated towards one another at the party. John Sasso says he remembers that I talked about how much I enjoyed fundraising. He had met a lot of people who raised political money with varying degrees of competence and some people who were quite good at it but he had never before met a single person who said he actually enjoyed it. We met again for dinner at the famous Parker House near the State House in Boston. He told me then something that I never forgot. He said, ``Bob, politics is a tough business. You survive by making friends, not enemies.'' That is not only a motto I live by but I repeat it to every candidate I support. John is the smartest political operative I ever met. He grew up in New Jersey and came to Massachusetts to attend Boston University and like many students, including me, never left. We became friends and in early January, Mike Dukakis asked me to be the finance chairman of his campaign.

That was also the beginning of my friendship with Mike and Kitty Dukakis. Kitty and I hit it off right away. Kitty and Mike Dukakis were parodied beyond recognition by the opposition in the 1988 presidential campaign. She is a warm and caring woman. Kitty was the daughter of Harry Ellis Dickson, the famous associate conductor of the Boston Pops. Mike and Kitty are a classic case of opposites attracting. She is as outgoing as Michael is reserved. He is notoriously parsimonious. Kitty has no trouble spending money and one of her standard phrases is ``don't tell Michael'' about a new dress or pair of shoes. If he noticed something new, she always insisted it was some old thing she dug out of the back of her closet.

I was so dismayed to learn that Michael owned only two business suits during the campaign that I persuaded a donor to contribute a bolt of cloth and had two nice suits tailored for him. Michael bought his suits off the rack in the famous

A NEW BEGINNING

original Filenes Basement in downtown Boston. The stories about him dive bombing for bargains during the Brooks Brothers annual sale are legendary in Massachusetts. But the stories overstate his interest in anything remotely related to sartorial elegance and speak more to his notorious frugality.

When she met Michael in the early 1960's, Kitty was a divorced mother of a young son. The difference in religion (she is Jewish and Michael is Greek Orthodox) and her circumstances as a single mother did not deter Mike. They fell madly in love and remain deeply in love to this day. They have one of the strongest marriages I have ever seen and in political circles that is rare. He adopted her son John who took his name and they had two beautiful daughters, Andrea and Kara.

Kitty, like many political spouses, spent many evenings alone. Political duties took Michael out several nights a week and their children were grown enough to be busy with their own activities and lives. Going along with him was not much fun. Political spouses are virtually ignored at political events. The public wants to meet the candidate so the wives have to fend for themselves, look attractive and smile when introduced as `` his lovely wife" and listen to the same speech they have heard 50 times with some attentiveness. On nights when Michael had to campaign, Kitty and I would sometimes meet for dinner. She is a wonderful dining companion. And I have traveled with her all over the world including Thailand to visit refugee camps and Rome for the investiture of Bernard Law as Cardinal of the Archdiocese of Boston. She is extraordinarily generous with her compassion and time and has always devoted herself to helping refugees and people in need and has done some courageous work on issues related to her own addiction to alcohol and drugs.

John Battaglino, a good friend and fellow fundraiser who made his fortune building a chain of college book stores which he eventually sold to Barnes & Noble, and I accompanied her to a refugee camp on the border of Thailand and Cambodia. Kitty was a member of the Task Force on Cambodian Children and wanted to help the displaced children who had lost their families. A refugee living in Lynn, Massachusetts had asked Kitty to find her 14 year old brother who was believed to be in that camp. The young refugee came from a family of nine and had lost all her siblings except for this one boy. She had heard that the governor's wife was involved in the Task Force but she had no idea how to contact her. The young woman stopped cars with Dukakis bumper stickers at a traffic circle in Lynn until she found one driven by someone who knew the governor. He told her how to reach Kitty.

On that trip, Kitty was seated by herself in the First Class cabin and she wanted us with her so she told the airline people we were her ``security'' and needed to be with her. We were upgraded to First Class and subsequently identified ourselves as her ``security'' much to everyone's amusement.

A NEW BEGINNING

Later in the refugee camp, John and I walked on either side of her. The joke of being ``security" aside, we did worry that something might happen to her. She was so passionate about the cause that she ignored routine safety precautions and if something happened to Kitty, Michael would have both of our heads. She was able to track down the boy through a priest at the refugee camp and got him back to Massachusetts and reunited with his sister about six months later. A family in Lynnfield took in the boy and his sister. He graduated from the public high school in Lynnfield and then won a full scholarship to Brandeis University in Waltham. He became a registered nurse and is the only member of the staff at Lowell General Hospital who speaks Khmer.

At another point in that trip, we stayed in a compound in a rural area where all the houses were on stilts. After dinner and a lot of beer, we returned to our rooms for the night. Kitty woke in the nighttime and needed to use the lavatory but was afraid she might open the wrong door in the dark so she went outside. As she squatted down to do her business, the dogs started barking wildly and every light in the place went on. We all had a good laugh about that afterwards.

One day Kitty and I were driving from Brookline to downtown Boston, and I told her I was gay. She said, ``Don't tell Michael." She said my sexual orientation was not a subject he would feel comfortable discussing but she would tell him for me. It was never an issue with him and over the years, he became more comfortable with the subject so we now joke about it.

One night, Tim McNeill and I were joining three other couples including Mike and Kitty for dinner. The hostess had arranged for the guests to be seated by gender, the usual boy, girl, boy, girl arrangement, but then stopped when she realized Tim and I were both men. She shrugged and said, ``Hey, we're here to eat... not to breed.'' It was a funny moment that showed how attitudes towards gay couples were changing even then.

One day Mike and I were traveling in western Massachusetts. We stayed overnight in Williamstown at the home of Kitty's father, Harry Ellis Dickson who was the conductor of the Boston Pops for more than 40 years. We stopped at a Friendly's for breakfast and Mike went to grab the newspapers. The Boston Herald, the tabloid, had a huge headline blaring ``Duke Trips over Sex Tapes.'' We were incredulous. No one is more proper than Michael Dukakis. I remember the very idea of Dukakis being involved in any sexual escapade was hilarious to me. To this day, Mike insists it was no laughing matter.

It was a convoluted story. Apparently, a Dukakis campaign volunteer, not a paid staffer, made a parody of an Ed King radio ad that featured Governor King's wife Jody making a testimonial in favor of her husband. The parody was in very bad taste. Sasso made the mistake of playing it for a reporter on an off the record basis as a joke. The King campaign found out and Governor King went public with an

A NEW BEGINNING

explosive demand that Dukakis apologize for dishonoring his wife. The whole matter blew over very quickly. Mike had never even heard about the parody. But it was a revelation to me to see something that had virtually nothing to do with the candidate attract so much attention in the media.

I made friendships on that first campaign that last until this day. I have made friends in every campaign that I worked upon. There is something about the bunker mentality of a political campaign that encourages lasting ties. Sharing a cause and experiencing the roller coaster of highs and lows of a political campaign forges bonds between people. And it also suits my personality. As I said before, I really like and enjoy people.

The Dukakis gubernatorial campaign set up shop in the Park Plaza Office complex in downtown Boston just a block away from the Boston Public Garden. The office building was a bit down on its heels at the time which made the rent very affordable for a campaign. It was well positioned near subway stops and a short walk to the State House where many of the state political reporters worked. Most campaigns are bare bones operations with rented or borrowed second hand furniture and, at the beginning, only a few staff people. The Dukakis campaign started with a small suite that included an office for Sasso, an office for the campaign finance staff which included the supremely competent Kristin Demong, the finance director who became one of my dearest friends, and a room for the volunteers

◄ **THE MONEY GUY**

who came in every day to stuff envelopes and make phone calls. Campaigns always start very small with a tiny core of basic staff and they grow like topsy at an extraordinary pace. As the campaign progresses, more and more people become involved and the number of employees and volunteers explodes. The campaign then grows from a few offices to a floor of a building, then two floors and sometimes, as in the Dukakis presidential campaign in 1988, consumes the entire building. Managing this rapid growth takes considerable skill.

I never tried to interfere with the operation of the campaign because I was not the campaign manager and I felt that job was far beyond my expertise. But I did make certain that the key fundraisers felt appreciated and engaged in the campaign. I asked Sasso to meet regularly with my key people and brief them. I was not going to tell him what to say or not to say but I wanted my people to feel as though they were on the inside of the campaign. They wanted to feel connected to the campaign. John understood that and never stinted on finding time to meet with the finance committee members.

I developed the template that I built upon for subsequent campaigns. Basically, I began to build concentric rings of supporters. Not everyone can raise $100,000 but nearly everyone can raise about $5,000 or sometimes $10,000 from friends, relatives and business associates. And that campaign focused on small donors as well. A working person who gives a candidate $25 is really committed because that $25 is meaningful money if you don't have much. I often compare it to the $2 betters at a race track. I've never gone to a race track where somebody who bet $2 on a horse did not root for that horse all the way around the track. The Dukakis campaign layered its field organizing with small donor fundraising because of the belief that someone giving hard cash would make certain to get to the polls on Election Day and would probably bring their friends and relatives along with them. That small donation represented political commitment and votes.

I learned a lot on that campaign. We never hosted fundraising dinners, for example, because it was really obvious that donors would rather mix and mingle and visit than eat a tired old chicken dinner and be stuck at a table all night listening to hours of droning speeches. We saved a lot of overhead by hosting cocktail parties. The contributors were much happier if they had a drink and could work the room and talk to friends. And most donors would rather their money be spent on something worthwhile, like campaign ads or brochures or whatever else the campaign needed to get its message out to voters. A dinner involved a lot of overhead and ate up precious dollars needlessly.

The one exception to this rule was the dinners I held for members of the finance committee in the big family room we called Elsa's Revenge at the house in Brookline. The prior owner of the house had strayed from his marital vows and his wife Elsa built that room onto the house after she discovered he had been unfaithful. We could fit 35 people

THE MONEY GUY

comfortably for dinner in that room and I hosted many dinners for finance committee members to encourage them to bond with one another and make certain they felt valued.

One evening I hosted a number of prominent fundraisers from across the country. I asked Johnny Hayes, a Tennessee businessman who acted as finance chairman for each of Al Gore's campaigns, to introduce Michael at the breakfast the morning after the dinner. He stood up and said, ``We really had a fine dinna at Farmah's house last night. And some of us went out to a bar and continued drinkin'. Ah don't know what time we got in but when I put my shoes on this morning, they were still warm!" I loved that story. Johnny sadly lost his battle against cancer in 2008.

I also adopted Dukakis' very high standards. I realized that I had to be scrupulous in raising money for him. One day, John Battaglino hosted a fundraising event at his house in Waltham, a western suburb outside of Boston. He quietly handed me an envelope that contained about $500 in cash and explained that the money came from some businessmen who held state contracts. They wanted Dukakis to beat Ed King but they were reluctant to be known publically as Dukakis supporters because it might cost them their state contracts and anger the sitting governor.

Afterwards, I took that envelope out of my pocket and showed it to Dukakis. He ordered me to turn the car around and we drove back to John's house and handed it back to him. Michael was pristine. Every contributor to

A NEW BEGINNING

his campaign had to be identified and he was not going to accept a single dollar anonymously.

A man named Paul C. Porter had made a name for himself by raising money for virtually every major Democratic candidate in Massachusetts in 1978. He wanted to host an event for Michael for the rematch campaign. Dukakis spotted him at one of our finance committee meetings and quietly advised me to make sure he never saw that man again at another Dukakis campaign meeting. I had no idea what the issue was. Porter had seemed like a pleasant enough guy. But Dukakis had an uncanny instinct for trouble and illegality. The following year Porter was arrested and charged with conspiracy to purchase $2 million in marijuana from federal undercover agents. A federal appeals court eventually overturned the conviction on a technicality but the point was well taken. Had Porter been involved in the campaign, Porter's legal issues would have reflected poorly on Dukakis and his judgment.

Another man, Larry Reservitz, a disbarred lawyer who had been convicted and served time for bilking insurance companies, wanted to host a fundraiser for Dukakis. Reservitz grew up in Brockton, Massachusetts, the son of a lawyer and took over the family firm after his father's death. Dukakis said he would accept a contribution from Reservitz because he had paid his debt to society and apparently was living a law-abiding life but would not allow him to raise any money for the campaign.

Dukakis' instincts were flawless. Reservitz subsequently got

◄ THE MONEY GUY

caught up in the marijuana deal with Porter but he turned state's witness for the FBI to reduce his prison time and testified he tried to cash a bogus check for $2 million from the account of L. Ron Hubbard, the founder of the Church of Scientology. That deal got Larry put into witness protection but he was not done. He surfaced years later and was convicted of money laundering conspiracy in connection with a massive $3.5 billion Ponzi scheme in Minneapolis. At the age of 68, he was sentenced to jail for almost 11 years.

During the Dukakis campaign, Reservitz and Porter invited me to Brockton for a heavy weight championship fight. I was flattered by the invitation but I could not attend. I was lucky I did not go. That episode taught me an important lesson in how unscrupulous people can manipulate you. After that episode, I was extremely cautious about accepting invitations or favors from anyone I did not know well. I knew then that I could never know a stranger's true agenda.

I was fortunate to have worked with someone like Dukakis at the beginning of my political fundraising career because I was so naïve at the start, I may have made a mistake and gotten into some real trouble. No one would ever confuse me with Mother Teresa but I became very sensitive to the fact that people have different agendas. By absorbing Michael's high standards and scrupulous adherence to the letter of the law, I kept out of trouble in a business where a mistake can be politically fatal and even get you put in jail.

In 1978 when he was a sitting governor, the Dukakis campaign raised $665,000 for his campaign against Ed King.

A NEW BEGINNING

We raised more than $4 million for the rematch campaign of 1982. That campaign put me on the national map as a fundraiser.

We were all elated when Dukakis won the election in 1982. During his first term, Dukakis had refused to hire anyone from his campaign or reward supporters. He realized that was a little bit too pure after he lost the election in 1978 and when he returned to office in 1983 with John Sasso as his chief of staff, friends and supporters played active roles in the administration. Two parking spots at the rear of the State House were reserved for the governor's use. Dukakis rarely used more than one because he often rode the green line on the MBTA to and from Brookline to the Park Street Station just steps from the State House. I often brought people in to see him so I was allowed to use the other spot. It was a heady thing for me to pull into my own private parking spot at the State House.

During his second term, Dukakis wanted to maintain better relationships with businessmen from around the state so I suggested he host regular lunches at the governor's office. I had my own agenda. I knew I stood a better chance of recruiting those businessmen to the finance committee if they had established a relationship with the governor.

Those lunches were a win win proposition for the governor and the participants. At each lunch, everyone would be introduced, the Governor would talk and the participants would ask questions as they ate tuna fish sandwiches. It gave them an opportunity to be heard by the governor and

◄ THE MONEY GUY

it gave the governor a chance to explain his philosophy and positions to them face to face.

An invitation from the governor is a command performance. No one turns it down. It was a great way to build relationships. Those lunches gave us the opportunity to expand the network of fundraisers and also build political support for the governor's policies. It helped Dukakis understand the financial needs of business better and certainly generated a lot of appreciation among the business community for his skill and intellect and integrity.

Those lunches helped me replenish the ranks of the finance committee for the 1986 reelection campaign, too. As many as half of the committee members from 1982 had moved onto other things by 1986. That made me realize that the 1982 election had changed my life and changed the lives of Mike and Kitty but not really affected the day to day life of most of the fundraisers. I learned from that to constantly be on the look out for new finance committee members to replace those who lose interest or cannot stay involved.

With Dukakis back in office, my horizons continued to expand. Early in Dukakis' term as governor, Senator Ted Kennedy invited me to be his guest overnight as his house overlooking the Potomac River in McLean, Virginia. Senator Kennedy was the youngest son of a storied political family. His father Joseph was Ambassador to the Court of St. James. His mother Rose was the daughter of a legendary Boston Mayor, John `` Honey Fitz" Fitzgerald. His brother John was president. His brother Robert was Attorney

A NEW BEGINNING

General. The assassinations of John and Robert had made Ted the object of all the unrealized yearnings of millions of Democrats who wanted to see Democrats back in the White House.

Kennedy had mounted an unsuccessful primary challenge against President Jimmy Carter in 1980 but the hope still burned. When he invited me to visit, it was just the two of us in his living room. The room was filled with photographs of members of the Kennedy family. I subsequently came to learn that every office, every house that Kennedy owned was a defacto family museum loaded with photographs and mementoes from the family. Looking at those famous faces, I remember thinking, ``I am 44 years old. What am I doing here!"

Kennedy and I sat in the living room and we each had a Scotch and he started to make the case of how and why he should be the next President of the United States and why I should help him do it. I was pinching myself. I had been the finance chairman for Mike Dukakis in Massachusetts but this was someone I was simply awed by. His first name was ``Senator". This guy could be the next President of the United States and he is trying to sell me on it. Who am I! Kennedy asked me to be involved in his next campaign and I said I would be honored. He then asked me to meet with his brother in law Stephen Smith who lived in New York City. Steve Smith was married to Ted's sister Jean and was responsible for handling the finances for the entire Kennedy family. He had been the finance chair of

THE MONEY GUY

John Kennedy's presidential campaign and managed the presidential campaigns of Robert and Ted Kennedy. He was probably the most important family member the public never heard much about. He was a character. At the end of every phone conversation, Steve just slammed down the phone and never said goodbye. When he finished saying what he wanted to say, he put down the phone and that was it.

A week after that visit, it was announced that Robert Farmer had been named national treasurer of Ted Kennedy's campaign. A week after that, Kennedy announced he would not run for President in 1984. One of my cousins called me and said he had just heard my name mentioned on the national news. In reporting Kennedy was not running for President, the television commentator said Bob Farmer must be very disappointed.

Kennedy changed his mind because of his children. Senator Kennedy's long troubled marriage to Joan Kennedy was over but he remained devoted to his three children, Kara, Ted Jr. and Patrick who was then still a teenager. Over the Thanksgiving Day holiday weekend, all three children weighed in very strongly against another presidential campaign. They had lost two uncles and did not want to lose their father. He acceded to their wishes and never again ran for the presidency but he did become one of the most powerful United States Senators in American history until his death from brain cancer in 2009.

One of the things I remember best about Ted was his ability

A NEW BEGINNING

to use self deprecating humor. Someone once told me that an audience will rarely remember much of what you said, but that at the end of the day they will remember whether they liked you or disliked you.

I ended up hosting a lot of parties for the Senator's Political Action Committee which many Senators use to help other candidates running for public office. The dinners were very intimate affairs at Kennedy's house in McLean involving about eight or ten people who would pay $5000 each for the honor of attending. Frank Keefe, the Secretary of Administration and Finance in Dukakis' second term, was scheduled to attend one dinner but failed to show. I was very concerned because there were so few guests and I had guaranteed Kennedy's committee a specific amount of revenue from the evening.

It turned out that Frank hopped in a taxicab at Washington's National Airport and asked to be taken to the Senator's house in McLean but the cab driver mistakenly overshot the house and took him instead to the better known Hickory Hill estate several miles away where Kennedy's sister in law, Ethel Kennedy lived. Frank was escorted to the library and Ethel arrived and chatted with him. She finally realized he was in the wrong place and called him a cab to take him to the Senator's place. Frank arrived half way through dinner.

Kennedy appreciated the fundraising I did on his behalf. Every year he invited me to be a guest at the Kennedy Center Honors, one of the most sought after social events

◄ THE MONEY GUY

in Washington, D.C. Each year a group of iconic American performing arts stars are honored for lifetime achievement. I met a lot of celebrities and Hollywood stars at that event. The Senator threw a cocktail party at the house in McLean just before the event and we would all go together to the Kennedy Center for the Performing Arts for the spectacular show which is always taped and broadcast on television afterwards.

Kennedy was special. He understood human nature as well as any one I have ever met. Bill Clinton also had that acute understanding of people but he did not reach out to people the way Kennedy did time after time. Kennedy also got me involved with the John F. Kennedy Presidential Library. John Cullinane, a very successful Massachusetts businessman who served as chairman of the board of the John F. Kennedy Library Foundation, recruited me to be president of the Foundation.

Cullinane created the first successful software products company in the world and made a tremendous amount of money when it went public, the first software company to go public with an IPO. He has been very generous with his fortune. I helped the Foundation raise millions of dollars to endow the library which is located on a peninsula just between South Boston and Dorchester sticking into Boston Harbor. I was honored to be asked to help contribute to such a worthy project.

That experience taught me the difference between fundraising for a campaign and fundraising for a charity. In political

A NEW BEGINNING

fundraising, you are looking for $1,000 or $5,000. The dollars are much higher when doing charitable fundraising.

When raising money for the Kennedy Library, Bill Brown, the chairman of the Bank of Boston, and I would go to corporate offices and tell potential donors about the library and how it would benefit the city. One day we pitched Norman Leventhal, the real estate magnate. He readily agreed to give $75,000 over the next five years. The very next week, Norman called Bill and asked him to support a park he was building in downtown Boston. Bill offered $100,000 over five years. I discovered you want to solicit board members for either a charity or a campaign who control large corporate donation accounts or who are so wealthy they routinely give away large amounts of their own money. Every corporation has a line item for charitable giving and CEO's routinely donate to one another's favorite causes.

One time I took Helen Spaulding as a date to a black tie Kennedy Library event. Helen's husband Si died suddenly of a heart attack in 1983 at the age of 60. Helen said, ``It will be so nice to see Jackie again.'' I was startled. ``You know Jackie Kennedy?'' I asked. ``Of course,'' she replied, ``She was in my wedding.'' I was stunned. I had known Helen for years and never known of this connection. ``She was in your wedding?'' I said sounding like a broken recording. And Helen said, ``Well, I was in hers.'' It says something about the discretion of old New England families that Helen had never once mentioned she was so close

◄ **THE MONEY GUY**

to Jackie Kennedy that they had been in one another's wedding parties.

Being chairman of Kennedy's presidential campaign for a week raised my profile nationally. Other candidates began to approach me. Mike Dukakis was supporting Walter Mondale who had been Jimmy Carter's vice president. Mondale was considered the favored candidate, the establishment candidate in 1984 and he ended up winning the nomination. I was invited to New York to dine with Jim Johnson, Mondale's right hand man who later became the chairman of Fannie Mae, and Robert Rubin, the financier who later became Treasury Secretary. They invited me to accompany Mondale on a trip to Iowa. I very much liked Mondale. He was a very warm and nice person. I got him aside at one point and told him that I thought he needed to know I was gay. He said, `` Bob, it is my experience that if gay people can share that with friends, they feel more comfortable with themselves. It makes no difference to me."

That story was told in a slightly different way in Terry McAuliffe's memoir. In the telling Nate Landow, a Maryland fundraiser and the head of IMPAC88, said that Mondale came up to him and said he had the strangest conversation with Bob Farmer. Mondale allegedly said, ``I don't know what he was doing in my closet, but he came out of the closet." It was not precisely true but it was a pretty funny story nonetheless.

Landow hoped to keep the group of Mondale fundraisers

A NEW BEGINNING

together to support the same candidate in 1988. I brought Dukakis down to speak to the group and he did a terrific job. But the group ended up endorsing Al Gore. And later, Gore privately told me the group had been less than effective. I learned you cannot get an eclectic group of national fundraisers with all the different individual relationships to agree on one candidate. Everyone is going to do his own thing.

My good friend Mike Berman was treasurer of the Mondale campaign and there really wasn't a job available for me. All the spots were already taken. I could have just stayed in Massachusetts and raised money for Mondale there but I wanted to play a role in a national campaign and expand my horizons so I kept looking for a campaign where I could play a leadership role.

I was interested in John Glenn, the Senator from Ohio, my home state, and the first American to orbit the earth in space. Glenn was a genuine American hero, a straight shooting military man in the tradition of Dwight D. Eisenhower. He was a decorated World War II Marine Corps combat pilot and one of the nation's first astronauts. I spoke to Glenn's campaign manager Bill White and told him I wanted to be national treasurer of the presidential campaign. I was invited to a party in Washington hosted by Tommy Boggs, the famous lobbyist, which Glenn and his wife, Annie, attended. Glenn invited me to drive back into town with him while Annie went back with Bill White. I said I'd like Annie to come with us so she got into the back seat.

THE MONEY GUY

I suspect he thought I was going to ask him to name me an ambassador when he became President but I had something a little more personal and private in mind. I needed to let him know I was gay before he named me to the position.

Glenn took the wheel of the car and I got in the passenger side of his car. As we drove along, I told him that I had wanted him to know I was gay. He did not say anything but he gripped the steering wheel so tightly his knuckles turned white. I was not at all sure what would come of this and suspected my job as his campaign treasurer might be short lived. He told me he would have to think about it and get back to me.

A week later, I received a telephone call from the Glenn campaign inviting me to be treasurer of his campaign. Glenn's daughter Lynn later told me that her father had never before met anyone whom he knew first hand was gay. He had unquestionably met gay people before but in his experience no one had ever identified himself as gay. This may seem incredible today when gay men and lesbians are able to be open about their orientation but men of his generation stayed in the closet. Glenn had been born in 1921 and spent much of his life in the macho Marine Corps military culture. I guess I must have helped broaden his horizons. I worked out an arrangement with the Glenn campaign to pay my expenses and flew to Washington to essentially work fulltime raising money for his campaign.

One day John Camp, a lawyer lobbyist with ties to the

oil industry and a member of Glenn's finance committee, approached me. He had just heard that I was gay. Camp called me to say, ``Mr. Farmer, I think you would serve John Glenn better if you went back to Massachusetts and raised money for him up there.'' It was the one time in my political career that someone confronted me over being gay. Of course, I paid no attention to him.

I did become great friends with Glenn's daughter Lynn and his wife Annie. Annie was a very warm person and she suffered from a severe stutter which made everyone who knew her feel very protective towards her. One day at an event at Brandeis University in Waltham, Massachusetts, a student asked Glenn for his position on gays in the military. The policy was very firm back then: no gays were allowed to serve in the U.S. military. The ``don't ask don't tell'' policy did not go into effect until almost ten years later during the Clinton administration. When the student asked the question, Annie grabbed for my hand and held it. It was a very characteristic gesture on her part. She wanted to make certain I would not take his answer personally.

During that campaign, I was interrupted one day during my regular gin rummy game. I was the only non-Jew in the game. The call was from John Glenn and he asked if I he was calling me at a good time. I looked around the table and said, ``Actually Senator, I am in a meeting with some Jewish leaders, can I call you back?'' Every time since then, I always say I am in a meeting with Jewish leaders when a phone call interrupts a card game.

THE MONEY GUY

One day when I was heading to New York City to recruit fundraisers for John Glenn. I went to my friend Joe Grandmaison and said, "Joe, I'm going to New York to try and bring some Jewish leaders into the campaign. Do you have a list?" Joe said, "Bob, just get the New York telephone directory. Everyone considers himself a Jewish leader in New York."

I really liked John Glenn personally. But his campaign never did very well in a contest dominated by former Vice President Walter F. Mondale, Colorado Senator Gary Hart and civil rights activist Jesse Jackson. The Glenn campaign flamed out in Iowa before ever really gaining any traction. He received 3.5 percent of the vote. Even "uncommitted" did better at 9.4 percent. He always got more applause when he was introduced than he received after concluding his remarks. He was not a very compelling speaker. But he was a great human being and his campaign put me in the national mix. I traveled all over the country for John Glenn and met people whom I would work with again in future campaigns. A photograph I prize shows me sitting next to Glenn, a very expert pilot, in the cockpit of his plane. A great regret for me and a reason I caution candidates to never go into debt in a campaign was his campaign left him with a $3 million debt that took 20 years to pay off.

After the 1984 campaign ended, Dukakis was involved in the Democratic Governor's Association and asked me to become the treasurer and help raise money for Democratic governors and gubernatorial candidates across the nation.

A NEW BEGINNING

Getting me out on the national fundraising circuit would prove to be a beneficial experience for the 1988 Dukakis presidential campaign. Chuck Dolan, the executive director of the DGA, was one of the first people I met. Chuck came from a blue collar Irish Catholic family in Massachusetts. We took the same flight from a DGA meeting back to Washington and arranged to sit next to one another to talk on the flight and get to know one another better. We each ordered Scotch from the airline attendant and settled in for a long flight.

I told him, ``Chuck, we are going to be spending a lot of time together and you don't know me very well. There is something you ought to know: I'm gay.''

Chuck said it did not matter to him so long as I did not hit on him.

So I replied, ``How would you feel if I told you that you were not my type?''

Chuck said, ``Relieved!''

We both laughed and became great friends.

I hosted many people as guests when I was US Consul General to Bermuda and Chuck came down one time when the cook was off. I remembered Chuck had told me he worked as a short order cook to earn his way through college. I wanted to watch a football game with another guest, my friend Rodney who is British and gay so I asked

THE MONEY GUY

Chuck if he could rustle up some sloppy joes. Chuck put on an apron and started cooking and later said he was struck by how the conventional stereotypes were upended. He, the straight guy, was cooking in the kitchen while the two gay guys sat in the living room watching football and drinking. I have always had the same tastes as my straight friends: football, Scotch, cards and golf.

In hindsight, the early 1980's trained me for the big time and prepared me for the most important campaign of my life, the 1988 campaign when my good friend Mike Dukakis became the Democratic Presidential Nominee. Everything I learned in the John Anderson campaign, the 1982 gubernatorial rematch campaign, the 1984 Glenn campaign was just a warm up to 1988.

CHAPTER 5

The Father of Soft Money

A ringing telephone woke me from a sound sleep on the morning of March 16, 1987. It was still chilly in New England and I was enjoying the sunshine and warm weather at my condominium in Miami Beach. I grabbed the telephone and heard Kitty Dukakis' voice. Without even saying hello, she blurted out: ``We are running.''

I had been waiting for that call for a long time. And by the time Michael Dukakis decided to run for President I felt ready.

It had been apparent to me for a long time that he might seek the presidency in 1988. However, Dukakis made this decision in a careful methodical way, the way he always made major decisions. In his mind, running for president was never a foregone conclusion. Ronald Reagan's second term would end in 1988. Without an incumbent Republican in the White House, the Democrats had a better chance of winning the election. In mid-December of

THE MONEY GUY

1985, Senator Ted Kennedy announced he would not run in 1988 after his family once again strongly opposed another presidential campaign. Kennedy, as the senior senator from Massachusetts, had first dibs on a national campaign among Massachusetts politicians.

Dukakis' Chief of Staff John Sasso, the most brilliant political analyst I ever met, had been carefully plotting a national campaign since he returned from serving as the campaign manager for the 1984 vice presidential candidate, Geraldine Ferraro, the Democratic Congresswoman from Queens who was the first woman to run on a national ticket. He carefully elevated Dukakis' national profile through involvement in the Democratic Governor's Association (DGA) and shrewdly positioned his boss in the best possible way for a national campaign. The state's economy was booming, the so-called Massachusetts Miracle, and Dukakis' brand of pragmatic progressive politics played well across the country.

I played my own role in this process by serving as treasurer for the DGA and spent time getting to know all of the Democratic governors across the nation as well as their top fundraisers and hopefully honing the skills that would be called upon to raise the extraordinary amount of money needed for a presidential campaign.

The previous year, just before Labor Day of 1986, Michael had asked me over to his house and sat me down at his kitchen table to talk about money and a presidential campaign. I had thought a lot about this so his question did

THE FATHER OF SOFT MONEY

not come as a total surprise. I deeply admired Michael and knew of no one else who would make a better President. He wanted to know if I thought we could raise enough money for a credible national campaign.

I told him I thought we could raise $6.5 million including federal matching funds by the time of the Iowa caucuses in 1988. That night, I had a hard time sleeping. I worried that I may have been too optimistic and I called him back the next morning and said ``Mike, I'm troubled about one thing.'' He said, ``What's that.'' And I told him ``I've never raised money for a guy who's at 1 percent in the polls before, and I don't know how it translates.'' Michael said he thought I raised a legitimate concern.

In any case, Michael focused on his reelection campaign as governor in 1986 and refused to commit to a presidential campaign or even seriously consider it until after Election Day in 1986. He did not have much of a race for his third term in Massachusetts but no smart politician plans the next campaign until the current campaign is finished and successful.

New York Governor Mario Cuomo posed the other major obstacle for a national run for Dukakis. Cuomo was one of the Democratic Party's most eloquent speakers and he and Dukakis were friendly and allies on many issues. In the 1988 cycle, Cuomo was the Hamlet of the Democratic field as he toyed with the notion for months. The media speculation was intense. The 1988 campaign certainly had room for one Northeastern liberal governor but not two. If

◄ THE MONEY GUY

Cuomo decided to run, Michael would not. At Michael's request I hosted a $50,000 fundraiser for Mario Cuomo at my home for Cuomo's campaign committee. Cuomo was charismatic, almost Lincolnesque. He spoke to a crowd in a way that made it sound like he was speaking to me personally. If he had decided to run, he would have been a formidable candidate. But Cuomo finally ended the vacillation in February of 1987 and took himself out of contention. With that announcement, the pace of the Dukakis' decision making process sped up.

Not five minutes after I hung up from Kitty's excited phone call, the phone rang again. It was Sasso. ``Get up here immediately,'' he said. I booked myself on the next flight and flew back to Boston from Miami that very afternoon and the campaign was underway.

On the flight, I thought about what it would take to put together the operation needed to raise money for a national campaign. The first thing I did was recruit Kristin Demong, the smartest and most competent manager I knew, to be finance director. I always believed that the finance director would hire the finance staff and my job as the chief fundraiser was to recruit members of the finance committee. Michael had virtually no name recognition around the country but he did have a few things going for him. The advantages included solid relationships with other governors although most were reluctant to endorse him right away until he showed he was a winner. His biggest advantage was he was the incumbent governor of Massachusetts, one of the ten most populace states, so he had the ability to tap into the considerable amount of political money available in the state. Every national campaign starts with the home state because the home state provides you with the seed money to take your message around the country. My first job was to establish a very strong Dukakis Presidential Finance Committee in Massachusetts. I came to appreciate that a supporter who might have raised $10,000 for the governor's race would probably raise $25,000 for a presidential race when he knows the candidate. A presidential race is on the front page of the newspapers every day not just in the state but in the big national newspapers such as the New York Times and Washington Post. That attention drives up interest. When a home town guy runs for the presidency and people begin to think ``My gosh this guy I've known for 10 or 20 years might change his name to Mr. President" and they get really excited.

I learned to never underestimate the power of a presidential campaign to excite interest and passion among the locals.

I took a suite at Le Meridien, an elegant hotel on Franklin Street in downtown Boston owned by the Leventhal family, prominent real estate developers, and set up my operation. The campaign staff set up appointments for me. Between 10 and 12 people a day came to the suite for about 30 minutes each. We'd have a cup of coffee and talk about the campaign and their friendship with Michael Dukakis. The Leventhals gave us the Presidential Suite at a terrific rate. It looked presidential. When potential supporters walked

THE MONEY GUY

into the suite and saw staffers bustling around serving coffee and answering the constantly ringing telephones, they couldn't help but be impressed. I remember the president of a utility company brought in $10,000 in checks for Michael's campaign. He was a Republican but he and his team felt they needed to contribute because their governor was running for President.

Early in the Dukakis campaign, I understood it was important to stage a major fundraising event that would be a major success. It would not only inspire the fundraising team but it would help establish Dukakis as a serious contender in the eyes of the national media.

We scheduled the first big fundraiser at the Park Plaza Hotel in Boston for April of 1987. The original goal was to raise $1 million. At that time, $1 million was considered a huge amount of money to raise in a single night. I wanted this fundraiser to be even bigger so I made a public announcement that we would raise $2 million. Kristin Demong, the campaign's finance director, almost had a nervous breakdown. She was furious with me for setting the bar too high. If we failed to reach the stated goal, even by a small amount, the fundraiser would be perceived as a failure. I'm a gambler but I felt really confident in making this bet. I had confidence in our team and believed in the candidate. And I knew we would exceed that $2 million goal. I never would have said $2 million if did not think we would beat it.

What I did not anticipate is the fundraiser took on a life of

THE FATHER OF SOFT MONEY

its own. There is a thrill and excitement about the presidential campaign of a local candidate and the energy and excitement in Massachusetts reflected the high esteem in which people of Massachusetts held their governor.

I had a strategy for this event to make certain our people performed at the highest possible level. Nothing is more important than making certain key fundraisers feel valued and appreciated. The Park Plaza event was so huge I worried that our finance committee members might feel they did not get full credit for the hard work they did in selling tickets if everyone was just lumped together in the huge ballroom. So I set up a series of smaller side rooms for fundraisers who brought in at least $50,000 and arranged for Governor Dukakis to visit each room and say a few words to the smaller groups before he addressed the big ballroom. The fundraisers appreciated the gesture. They got credit for their efforts from the governor and looked good in front of their friends and associates who ponied up the money. Part of my job was to make sure the candidate knew who was doing what and who was NOT doing what.

The Park Plaza event was the biggest event I had ever done. When I walked into the ballroom, a bank of television cameras lined the back of the hall. We had a huge overflowing press section for the large press contingent which included national reporters. We raised almost $4 million that night and everyone was just knocked out by the achievement. All three network affiliates in Boston interviewed me and put me on the air that night.

◄ **THE MONEY GUY**

The fundraiser put Dukakis firmly on the map as a player. From day one, Dukakis was the candidate with plenty of money. He reported $4.5 million in donations for that first quarter, far more than any other candidate in the race. By the time of the Iowa caucuses, the Dukakis campaign had raised $17 million, way more than the $6.5 million I predicted sitting at Michael's kitchen table 18 months earlier.

I knew a lot of people and had met a lot of fundraisers around the country through the Democratic Governors Association but after that first quarter report hit the headlines, just about everyone returned my telephone calls. The amount we raised piqued interest. They realized that Dukakis had a real shot. No one else was raising this kind of money. That was a turning point for our campaign. We capitalized on our success with an ``ambassadors'' program. And Dukakis got more invitations to speak at major party dinners and established his credibility as a serious candidate.

To raise money for a national campaign, I realized we had to expand our band of brothers who had worked together on the finance committee for the 1982 and 1986 gubernatorial campaigns.

I recruited Alan M. Leventhal, a member of the prominent real estate family, who was then in his mid-30's. I met Alan and his father Norman, during the Glenn campaign. They had raised more than $100,000 for Glenn in 1983 which was a lot of money at that time. Alan is one of the most talented and able people I know as well as incredibly energetic and eager to help. He turned out to be a natural powerhouse of a fundraiser. We became close and talked on the phone constantly every day. Alan eventually became the chairman and CEO of Beacon Properties Corps, one of the largest real estate investment trusts in the United States and is now chairman and CEO of Beacon Capital Partners. I thought Alan would be a valuable addition to the team because I discovered real estate developers had tremendous numbers of contacts. A developer could just call up his lawyers, accountants, contractors, and all of his other vendors and ask them to support the candidate. Trust me, no one would refuse. I asked him to be the national finance chairman. Alan had relationships and acquaintances all across the country. But more important, he exhibited a joie de vivre that made him a delight to be around.

Two valuable members of the old guard; my friends John Battaglino and Lenny Aronson who owned a real estate management company, went to Michael and complained that the campaign no longer felt like a family. I understood their resistance to change. They had been with Mike early and were stalwarts and saw the expansion of the campaign as threats to their influence and standing. But to succeed, we needed more people. The Governor recognized the need to expand the circle. Eventually, the flap blew over.

I created an ``ambassador's'' program to send members of the finance committee to states where the member had friends, relatives or business associates. Prominent

◄ **THE MONEY GUY**

fundraisers for presidents often end up being named to key ambassadorial positions after their candidate takes office but that was not the reason I chose the name. I felt these talented successful people were truly our ambassadors from Massachusetts to other states. There was never any quid pro quo on any Dukakis campaign. Of course everyone realized that practically speaking, the friends and supporters of the President were the ones he would call upon to serve in his administration. With the benefit of hindsight, it is interesting how many of these fundraisers ended up serving as U.S. envoys throughout the world years later during the Clinton and Obama administrations. It speaks to their talent and high quality.

So the Dukakis' team scattered throughout the country. Cathy Douglas Stone, the charming and committed environmentalist and widow of Supreme Court Justice William O. Douglas who moved to Boston after marrying James Stone, Dukakis' first insurance commissioner, went to her late husband's home state of Washington. We sent out Bob Epstein, a quiet and somewhat shy man who should never be underestimated as a person of drive and ability. He now owns the Boston Celtics. Bob went to Texas. His lovely wife Esther went to Vermont. Dick Morningstar, a brilliant business lawyer and tactician from Brookline, went to Arkansas and got to know the Clintons so well Dick later became the US Ambassador to the European Union during the Clinton Administration. Jon Rotenberg, a former state representative from Dukakis' home town of Brookline who had worked on Soviet Jewry issues, went to Florida where he sold yachts in Miami and Palm Beach. Jon is man of tremendous dignity and loyalty and a natural politician. Fred Alpert, a furniture store owner from southeastern Massachusetts, traveled frequently to North Carolina to purchase furniture for his store so he became the Dukakis campaign ambassador to North Carolina. George Danas, a Waltham Businessman, and Peter Bassett, a delightful comrade in arms and hotelier who then owned a number of Holiday Inn franchises, started to work the Greek-American community. Ron Ansin, one of my best friends, went to New York and began to develop a fundraising team in New York. Cream rises to the top in fundraising and Ron identified a real star in Nadine Hack, the wife of Jerry Dunfey, a member of the well regarded hotel management family from New England, who became finance chair in New York. My good pal Lenny Aronson went to Connecticut and John Battaglino ended up in California in a somewhat unexpected way.

I traveled to Los Angeles with Kitty Dukakis on an early fundraising trip and I knew John Battaglino was in Las Vegas to watch a championship fight. John had sold his six book stores to the Barnes & Noble chain by then so he had more free time. I called him and invited him to join us in LA for a few days, ``John,'' I said, ``you'll have more fun with me and Kitty.'' John had never been to California. After a few days accompanying us to meetings with potential supporters, Kitty and John prepared to fly back to Boston on a morning flight. As they stood by the hotel elevator with their bags, Kitty asked him if he would stay for a bit longer

◄ **THE MONEY GUY**

to see if he could get more results for the campaign. Poor John did not leave the state for 15 months.

John started cold calling prospects. His first visit to a potential donor showed him how little he knew about California. He remembers he stayed at the Beverly Wilshire Hotel and a potential donor told him his office was ``just up the street''. John grabbed his brief case and started walking dressed in a business suit with a carefully knotted necktie. Four miles later in 90 plus degree heat, he understood what Angelinos meant by ``just up the street.'' He ended up raising $5 million for the primaries for Dukakis in California, more than double the amount Mondale raised in the state as a former vice president four years earlier, and raised even more for the general election.

A lot of people were surprised we sent John to California. He was a plain spoken Massachusetts businessman from a humble background but he became a fundraising legend in California.

John tells me that he believes our fundraising team was successful because it was made up of self-made men and women of considerable maturity and experience. Each fundraiser oozed the self-confidence that comes from a lifetime of personal achievement and success and each had a compelling personal story of achievement to tell those he or she met. Moreover, our team was made up of volunteers who were in this fight because they admired Dukakis and wanted their friend and governor to

THE FATHER OF SOFT MONEY

be President of the United States. Few were looking for a pay back. In my experience, no one is more persuasive than a true believer. This gave them a lot of credibility with other successful business people.

John worked very hard to set up a meeting with Walter Shorenstein, probably the biggest fish in the pond in California. Shorenstein came back from military service during World War II and, as he told the story, started out his career with a pregnant wife and $1,000 in his pocket. He eventually became the biggest landlord in San Francisco and a hugely successful commercial real estate developer. He died in 2010 at the age of 95.

During his lifetime, Shorenstein enjoyed a reputation as a philanthropist and generous donor to Democratic presidential candidates dating back to Lyndon B. Johnson in the 1960's. So when John arranged the meeting, he asked me to join him to improve the odds we would be able to catch this big fish. As we walked down the hallway, I noticed a framed copy of an invitation to a State Dinner at the White House. We walked into Shorenstein's enormous office overlooking the bay in San Francisco. Shorenstein acted like he owned the place which he did. He sat at the head of his conference table in his suspenders with his jacket off. I delivered my standard pitch.

``Mr. Shorenstein, we all know how helpful you have been to Democrats in the past and we want you to be part of this effort. We believe Michael Dukakis is the candidate who can win this year. We want you to be with

THE MONEY GUY

us." He showed considerable reluctance to commit at this early stage. But I persisted, I said, ``the train is leaving the station."

He stood up and said, Mr. Farmer, I can buy my own f... train." He was very plain spoken.

Walter Shorenstein had his own agenda. He did not support the Dukakis campaign until after Michael won the Democratic nomination.

John tells another great story about a meeting Phil Angelides set up for him with two contributors in San Diego. Angelides was the son of Greek immigrants. He grew up in Sacramento and graduated from Harvard. After his work in the Dukakis campaign in 1988, he became chairman of the California Democratic state party and then state Treasurer of California. At this meeting he set up for John, the donors each handed John a check for $100,000. They claimed they only wanted a connection in the Dukakis campaign but John understood the winking and blinking going on and knew they expected much more

John accepted the checks and drove about a half a block before he turned around and went back to them and returned the two checks. He told them Michael Dukakis would never accept the checks under those circumstances and he could not do anything his friend would not do. The contractors were devastated but we all understood what Dukakis expected of us.

THE FATHER OF SOFT MONEY

Lew Wasserman, the talent agent and studio head, once offered John a check for $100,000 for the general election campaign. Those checks went to the Democratic National Committee for the general election campaign get out the vote effort. John did exactly what I would do, he said, "I don't want your check for $100,000. I want you to raise five checks for $100,000 from your friends." Wasserman introduced John to five of his friends and each one donated $100,000 to the national party. In this way, John brought another half a million dollars into the campaign.

One of the sources of the money was Greek-Americans. At the time, I had little appreciation for how powerful a draw Dukakis 'Greek heritage would be for other Greek-Americans.

People of Greek descent make up a tiny percentage of all Americans. In 1988, there were about one million Greek-Americans. It seemed as though most of them donated time or money to the Dukakis campaign in 1988. Both of Michael's parents were born in Greece. His father became a physician and his mother graduated from Bates College at a time few young women, never mind young immigrant women, acquired a higher education. Michael spoke Greek before he spoke English.

I am convinced every Greek pizza store proprietor regardless of party affiliation in America wrote a check to Michael. When Jon Rotenberg went to Florida for the campaign, he started out by systematically visiting Greek diners and says every one of them loved Michael and gave money. The

◄ **THE MONEY GUY**

Greek connection proved to be extraordinarily beneficial. One of our champions in the Greek community was Clay Constantinou, then a 37 year old lawyer in private practice in Colts Neck, New Jersey. Clay is undoubtedly the best natural fundraiser I have ever met in the business. He is indefatigable. I have seen him go out night after night around New Jersey to sit down with people and recruit them to his finance committee. He likes to meet people. Others were Phil Angelides in California who was then only 35 and Tasso Manessis, the owner of three restaurants in New York. Tasso was a little older. He was 52. The ethnic pride was palpable. Many Greek Americans were, like Michael, first generation Americans or immigrants like his parents. Tasso, for example, was born in Greece. Clay says that Greek Americans felt a real call to arms when Michael announced his candidacy. The community rose to the occasion to help elect one of their own to the presidency. Clay became our man in New Jersey. Four years later, he raised $4 million in New Jersey for Bill Clinton and Clinton named him US Ambassador to Luxembourg, a position he served with distinction for five years in the 1990's. Because Michael lost the election, Greek-Americans were less willing to help the next prominent Greek-American politician who ran for President, Paul E. Tsongas, the Senator from Massachusetts who ran in 1992. Paul's twin sister, Thaleia Tsongas Schlesinger, lived near me in Brookline. She was as outgoing as Paul was contained and she became a lifelong friend.

The ambassadors asked me what to do. I told them to visit

THE FATHER OF SOFT MONEY

the top elected Democratic officials in the state, the governor, big city mayors, members of Congress and say they were there as a courtesy call. I instructed the ambassadors in the basic pitch to potential givers, particularly those who might agree to serve on a campaign committee. It went this way. ``Governor Dukakis has heard of you because of your tremendous reputation. He wanted me to pay his respects because he very much wants to meet you. He is going to be coming here soon and wondered if you would like you to be on our host committee. When the Governor comes to town, we'd like you to ride in the car with him from the airport. We believe the Governor will be the next President of the United States and we think you ought to be on board.'' And I told them to be sure and ask each for the names of the top fundraisers in the state. Make a list of the local fundraisers and then visit each one. This is how we built a Dukakis campaign in states where no one had ever heard of him.

I had five people working directly for me: a chief of staff, a secretary, and a few people answering the phones and placing calls. Kristin Demong hired five regional finance directors and each assumed responsibility for a certain number of states. The regional finance directors were always very smart and very young. They would come to me with call sheets and sit in my office, dial the phone and brief me on who I was going to talk to and what the ``ask'' was. That is how I spent most of my time, calling people around the country and the way I ended every conversation was ``Thank you for your help or support. You are a great

◄ **THE MONEY GUY**

American." That phrase became my trademark. Through our ambassador program, I supervised about 25 lieutenants and each built a network in a different state or with a different constituency.

As the national treasurer I was often called by one of our ambassadors to help close a deal. I was able to do that because I got a lot of press. In most campaigns today, campaign staff is forbidden to talk to reporters. The campaigns want to control the message and speak with a single voice so the press secretary and maybe the campaign manager are the only people allowed to talk to reporters. I appreciate the need for message discipline but this always struck me as wrongheaded because the really good reporters will get people to talk off the record and a disgruntled staffer speaking anonymously can inflict great damage on the campaign. It always seemed to me that it made more sense to allow senior campaign staff to talk to reporters.

In my case, surprising myself, I became a ``personality''. There were a lot of headlines: stories:``Fund-Raisers Give Dukakis a Huge Edge'' in the New York Times March 22, 1988; ``the Dukakis Money Guy'' in the Boston Globe Nov. 10, 1985; ``Farmer with Green Thumb for Democrats Feted at 50'' in the Boston Globe Sept. 19, 1988;`` Farmer Makes Funds Grow'' in the Boston Globe March 18, 1988; ``Farmer with A Green Thumb'' in Time Magazine April 25, 1988;``Robert Farmer Soft Money Guy'' in the National Journal July 23, 2007.

Kirk O'Donnell, a brilliant political operative from Boston

THE FATHER OF SOFT MONEY

who worked for House Speaker Tip O'Neill and died far too young, called one day and told me "When you are working on a campaign as an operative and get a full page in Time Magazine, that is worth a cabinet position." This was the first time in my life I was a quasi public figure. I was amazed.

What I did not fully appreciate at the time was how much credibility those stories gave me. The coverage not only raised my profile with potential donors but suggested I had clout in the campaign. We raised the maximum then allowed by law for candidates accepting matching funds, $28.5 million, well before the primary season ended. Under the matching funds system, a candidate needed to raise $5,000 in amounts of less than $250 in 20 different states. I raised the $5,000 for Dukakis' rivals in Massachusetts as a gesture of good will. This was unusual. Al Gore, a 39 year old Senator from Tennessee making his first run for the Presidency that year, raised the $5,000 in Tennessee for Dukakis as a thank you. He was the only other candidate to do that and I always appreciated the gesture.

We broke all fundraising records that year. The deep pockets proved to be a huge advantage. The 1988 Democratic primary campaign was a war of attrition. At the beginning, there was no obvious leader. In fact, the field was often mocked as the Seven Dwarfs. The other candidates were Senators Joe Biden of Delaware, Paul Simon of Illinois, Al Gore of Tennessee and Gary Hart of Colorado; Civil Rights Leader Jesse Jackson; and Congressman Dick Gephardt of

◄ THE MONEY GUY

Missouri. Michael Dukakis had the resources to survive the rough primary campaign and become the Democratic Presidential nominee.

The fundraising achievement was significant in another way because we accomplished it by operating under more restrictions than the standard legal constraints. Michael Dukakis refused to take any money from political action committees (PACs) and registered lobbyists and limited state employee donations to $100. He also forbad us from systematically soliciting money from state contractors although an individual state contractor could donate money to the campaign on his or her own. He told me that I should assume that every single person I approached for a contribution would be interviewed by a reporter.

Michael had an uncanny instinct for trouble. Back during the 1982 rematch campaign against Ed King, Dukakis had insisted that no state employee give more than $100. I thought he was nuts. There was a survey supervisor at the state Department of Public Works named James W. Bougiokas who was from Haverhill, the city where Dukakis' mother Euterpe lived when she came to America. Bougiokas was also a Greek-American and he kept sending the campaign checks for $500. Michael always looked over the list of contributors and every time he spotted Bougiokas and his $500 check, he ordered that it be sent back. After Dukakis returned to the corner office at the State House, he started getting calls from members of the Greek community urging him to name Bougiokas Commissioner of

THE FATHER OF SOFT MONEY

the Department of Public Works. He never got that job. Dukakis did not think he was the best person for the position and not six months later, it came to light that Bougiokas was defrauding the state by funneling work to a private company he had set up. When the indictment was handed down, Dukakis called me and said, ``Bob, remember that guy who kept sending us the $500 checks? Well, he was just indicted. Listen to your friend, Dukakis!'' I learned to do just that.

After we raised money for the 1988 presidential primary campaign, my job was not done. We realized that an opportunity existed for our fundraising team to assist in raising money for the Democratic National Committee for the general election. Dukakis was surprised when he saw fundraising events on his schedule after the primary season. He thought we were finished and he could focus exclusively on campaigning for the presidency. I told him about ``soft money''. Dukakis was incredulous. The national party was allowed to raise almost unlimited funds. Dukakis didn't like the sound of that but I told him that he would be at an enormous financial disadvantage if we did not do all we could to help the national party. In 1984, Ronald Reagan raised about $50 million for the Republican National Committee and Walter F. Mondale, the Democratic nominee, only raised about $8 million for the Democratic National Committee. In addition to all the other challenges of that campaign, Democrats were at a huge disadvantage in financing the ground campaign that year.

◄ **THE MONEY GUY**

Dukakis relented. He was not going to be at a disadvantage. We raised $68 million for the Democratic Party's Campaign '88 fund which was used to finance the national field effort in a general election campaign. We convinced 148 individuals to write personal checks for $100,000 each and 140 others to raise $100,000 for the party. I came up with the idea of asking for $100,000. This had never been done before. You could buy a small condominium in Massachusetts for $100,000 but I knew a lot of people could afford it.

I ended up becoming famous as the father of soft money because of that innovation. A lot of people thought $100,000 was too much but Alan Leventhal and I visited Richard Cohen, the New York real estate developer, and made the ``first'' pitch. He said how much do you want and we said $100,000 and he said, ``Thank God ... I thought you were going to ask for more.'' That told us that there were enough donors able to give that kind of gift. Several wanted to give us more but we refused. It would have been counterproductive. By putting a cap on the amount, everyone was somewhat equal. If a $100,000 giver heard someone else gave more, he might feel that person was more important or had better access. For those of us who were close to him, the high point of the Dukakis campaign was his acceptance speech at the Democratic National Convention in Atlanta, Georgia. I had spent time with Mike and Kitty in their hotel suite that night watching the convention on television and enjoying dinner with them. We drove to the convention center in a caravan and Michael went behind the stage to await his cue and Kitty and I went to the section of the hall reserved for family. Michael entered the hall to the roar of Bruce Springsteen's anthem "*America*" and gave the best speech of his life. It is thrilling to see a close friend accept the nomination for the presidency of the United States. I will always be proud to be his friend and proud of the role I played in his campaign.

As the speech wound down, the staff fetched Kitty and escorted her backstage so she could join her husband at its conclusion. Then they came for me. I thought I was returning to the motorcade and followed the staff down a long corridor and up some stairs and people pushed me forward and suddenly there I was ... on stage behind Mike and Kitty. I stood arm and arm with Senator Lloyd Bentsen, the vice presidential nominee, and Ann Richards, the keynoter of the convention who was the state Treasurer in Texas and later became governor of the state. Everyone in the hall sang "*God Bless America*" and hundreds of cameras recorded the scene. It was just amazing. I could hardly believe I was there. I turned to Ann Richards and said, "You know, it doesn't get any better than this" ... Unfortunately, I was right. That was the high point of the campaign. Of course, the campaign was ultimately not successful. I always felt that the outcome might have been different if Dukakis had not allowed his campaign manager, John Sasso, to resign over something that with the benefit of hindsight was fairly benign.

Sasso discovered that Joe Biden had borrowed verbatim

◄ **THE MONEY GUY**

the text of a moving campaign speech delivered in the United Kingdom by a Labor politician named Neil Kinnock who had made an unsuccessful run against Prime Minister Margaret Thatcher. He got a copy of the video tape of Blair delivering the speech and had Paul Tully, a talented political operative well known in the party, leak it to Maureen Dowd of the New York Times, David Yepsen of the Des Moines Register and NBC News. Leaking damaging information about the opposition to the press is something campaign staffers do every day of the week. But this time it became a media firestorm. Michael was afraid it would hurt him in Iowa where voters expected campaigns to be super clean and this was somehow considered ``dirty politics''. The media was very good to me in that campaign but it can also be destructive. Michael felt he had to let Sasso go to stop the bad press. He never should have let Sasso leave the campaign. Sasso returned at the very end of the campaign but it was too late but by then the damage was done.

I remember the campaign ads run by the campaign of George H.W. Bush against Dukakis in 1988 vividly. The ads effectively defined Dukakis as a wild eyed liberal to millions of Americans who did not know anything about him. He was called ``a card carrying member of the ACLU'' as if being in favor of civil liberties and the Bill of Rights was a crime. There was an ominous ad on pollution of Boston Harbor that blamed Dukakis for hundreds of years of environmental degradation even though HE was the one who was cleaning it up. The Bush campaign exploited a

THE FATHER OF SOFT MONEY

prison furlough program that had been begun by Dukakis' Republican predecessor, Governor Frank Sargent. One of the lifers, an inmate named Willie Horton, escaped while on furlough and committed horrific crimes in Maryland before being arrested again. The Willie Horton case exploited people's fear of crime and racism and was used to make Dukakis appear weak on crime.

At the time, I dismissed the ads as farfetched. I knew Mike Dukakis and could not imagine that anyone would believe them. My mistake was in not appreciating that for those who did not know him at all, the ads painted him as risky choice for President. Michael was introducing himself to the country and those ads defined him as unacceptable. We all learned that no charge can go unanswered in a political campaign because ignoring the lie gives it credibility. It was a painful lesson.

Politics is a very tough business. Because of my proximity to powerful politicians, I was targeted by political enemies. The former US Attorney in Boston President Ronald Reagan's Attorney General, Edwin Meese, named Frank L. McNamara Jr. to be the chief federal prosecutor in Massachusetts in 1987. McNamara was a very conservative Irish Catholic lawyer who had run for Congress against House Speaker Thomas P. ``Tip'' O'Neill Jr. in 1982. In fact, that seemed to be his chief qualification for the job. He was only 39 at the time. He did not last too long. Twenty-eight of the 30 prosecutors in his office signed a letter demanding he resign two years after he

◄ **THE MONEY GUY**

took the job. He resigned within days of the letter becoming public.

While he was in office, he made a few wild charges. One was that he had seen the Republican Governor of Massachusetts William Weld who was his predecessor as US Attorney smoke marijuana at a party. But he could not prove it. Weld was considered a much more liberal Republican than McNamara who was deeply religious and the father of 12 children. The charge did not go down well with the career prosecutors in the US Attorney's office.

He also accused me and Joe Kennedy, the Democratic Congressman and oldest son of the late Attorney General Robert F. Kennedy, of being in cahoots with a marijuana drug dealer. The Boston Herald, the tabloid newspaper in Boston, ran a glaring headline *McNamara Accuses Joe K / Farmer in Pot Probe* with photos of all three of us on the tabloid cover. Joe Kennedy called me that morning after he saw the headline and said, ``Gee Bob, maybe we should have a *joint* press conference." We both laughed. The charge was baseless and it turned into a one day story that quickly disappeared.

I remember the Dukakis campaign fondly because I made so many lifelong friends at that time. Except for that one issue at the beginning when John Battaglino and Len Aronson complained we were expanding the campaign team too fast, there were literally no sharp elbows or infighting on the finance side of the Dukakis campaign. We had a lot of fun. One day I walked into the headquarters and saw Alan Leventhal wearing a shirt with a small hole. I stuck my finger in the hole and pulled making a big tear. Everyone joined in and started tearing at his shirt and pretty soon it was in total tatters. It was a silly moment but gives a sense of the camaraderie and fun we had during that campaign.

I am particularly proud of the fact that Mike Dukakis did not have to meet with more than five people or make more than five phone calls to raise money for his campaign. Our combined efforts allowed our candidate to focus on his job as a candidate and as a governor. I will always feel good about that.

CHAPTER 6

The Rainmaker

I spent the final night of the long 1988 presidential campaign on a cross-country non-stop campaign swing with Michael S. Dukakis. We began in California and ended in Massachusetts so the candidate could be home to vote. I played poker with the Secret Service agents on the small jet while the candidate slept. Our stops included an early morning tarmac stop in Iowa before a throng of local supporters. We finally landed at dawn in Boston and were greeted by another huge crowd. I was utterly exhausted so I went home and slept all day.

The election night party took place in the cavernous hall of the World Trade Center on Boston Harbor. I had a hard time accepting defeat. I could not believe we had come so far only to lose the election. Michael Dukakis held a 17 point lead over George H. W. Bush in August. It had evaporated into thin air and Michael lost by eight points. I was convinced Mike Dukakis would make a great President. But in politics, the best candidate does not always win.

THE RAINMAKER

Michael Dukakis' loss of the 1988 Presidential election ironically opened many doors for me. A number of things went wrong in his presidential campaign but the money side of the equation went exactly right. Dukakis never wanted for resources in that campaign and because I served as campaign treasurer, I was fortunate enough to get some credit for the fundraising success of our excellent team.

I had choices to make after that campaign. Dukakis offered me a job in Massachusetts as Secretary of Economic Affairs in his cabinet. I was flattered to be offered the position of overseeing the department which fostered economic development throughout the Commonwealth. He had appointed me to the State Board of Education and wanted me to serve as chairman but I resigned after two years because I just did not enjoy the politics of education. It was clear I had been bitten by the political bug and loved the national political scene. My exposure to national politics throughout the 1980's only made me want more involvement so Washington, D.C. beckoned.

I remember discussing my career dilemma with Barry Diller, the media mogul who became a close friend during the Dukakis campaign. I was a frequent houseguest of Barry's when I traveled to California. He had been CEO of Paramount Pictures before becoming chairman and CEO of Fox Inc. Barry told me to go to D.C.

But first I needed some time to recover. Tim McNeil and I drove from Massachusetts to Florida where we had a condominium. We stopped in Washington, D.C. on the

◄ **THE MONEY GUY**

way and some friends suggested I run for Treasurer of the Democratic National Committee. The idea appealed to me. I wanted to keep together the network of fundraisers from the Dukakis campaign. After financing the Dukakis primary campaign, many of these same fundraisers became Democratic Party ``trustees'' and raised a record amount of money for the party. But the incumbent Treasurer, Sharon Pratt Dixon, an African-American woman, wanted to run for reelection for another four year term. I wasn't sure I wanted to take her on.

Yet our fundraising success was still fresh in the minds of the party leaders. Members of the Dukakis finance committee wanted me to run and helped raise $200,000 for my campaign. That was a lot of money for a campaign for an internal party position in 1988. I hired Susan Brophy, a bright, extremely capable Massachusetts native who had held a senior position on the Dukakis campaign, to be my campaign manager. I flew around the country meeting with DNC members, the only people who could vote in this election. And it became very clear that this job was all about money and raising the resources to finance a party that was still out of power. With Republicans controlling the White House, the Democratic National Committee played an important role as the opposition and creating the best possible environment for a Democratic presidential candidate in 1992.

Ron Brown, a masterful Washington lawyer who had held senior jobs with both Senator Ted Kennedy and Rev.

THE RAINMAKER

Jesse Jackson, was running for party chairman. Paul Kirk, Kennedy's longtime friend and aide, decided not to seek reelection as chairman of the DNC. Ron was running against Richard Wiener, the Michigan state party chairman, and three U.S. Representatives, Mike Barnes of Maryland, James Stanton of Ohio and James Jones of Oklahoma. Ron approached me about running as a team but I demurred.

I told him, ``Ron, I'm running for treasurer. I don't know who is going to be chairman. I will support whoever is elected. It would not serve me well to commit to you and be estranged from the new chairman if you do not win.'' I liked Ron Brown. He was a very impressive and compelling man. But I needed independence so I could work comfortably with whoever won the race. With the benefit of hindsight, I may have been better off running with Ron but I made the best decision I could at the time. Ron later became the Commerce Secretary in Bill Clinton's cabinet, the first African-American to hold the position. He tragically died with 34 others during a trade mission to Croatia in 1996 when his Air Force jet crashed into a mountainside. It was a huge loss to the country.

In any case, Sharon Pratt Dixon saw the handwriting on the wall in our competition and withdrew from contention on the day of the vote. In fact, she spoke in favor of me. Sharon later became the first and only woman to ever be elected mayor of Washington, D.C.

Ron also won and we established a comfortable and strong working relationship. During my first meeting with him at his office, I made a number of requests for staff. I wanted to hire my own finance director for the party but Ron insisted upon hiring his own person and let me hire the deputy finance director. If I had endorsed him early and run with him as he asked, I suspect I might have been able to hire my own person. But we worked well together and traveled the entire country together. Raising money for the party out of power is always extremely difficult. We did OK, not great, but we did well enough to smooth the way for a Democratic presidential victory in 1992 and that was what mattered.

If I was going to be Treasurer of the DNC, I needed to live in Washington and I needed a day job. When I sold my business back in 1983, I did not anticipate needing money to maintain a home in Massachusetts as well as a residence in Washington, D.C. A real job would help pay the expenses of maintaining a residence in the District.

I had graduated from Harvard Law School many years earlier but never taken the bar examination because I never intended to practice law. This proved to be an obstacle at some major Washington law firms. But I never saw myself as a lawyer/lobbyist. I was not a policy wonk. I was a people person, a door opener, a salesman. My skills were recruiting talent and business, getting people together and creating the environment for a deal. I understood my strengths and weaknesses and my strengths clearly played to becoming a Washington rainmaker, a type of fixer. Craig Fuller, the chief of staff to George H. W. Bush, and I talked about setting up a bipartisan lobbying firm. Ann Lewis, Congressman Barney Frank's sister and a well known Democratic activist, suggested I talk to an up and coming investment banking group called the Carlyle Group. The Carlyle Group had been created the year before, in 1987, and eventually became one of the largest private equity firms in the world. With the benefit of hindsight, the Carlyle Group would have been a natural home for me.

But I signed on with Cassidy & Associates, the lobbying powerhouse founded by Gerald Cassidy, because they offered me the most money and Cassidy was the biggest lobbying firm in town. At the time, many people asked me if my potential employers were ``nice''. My experience is that all people are nice and if you deliver for them, they will be even nicer. If you do not deliver, it doesn't matter how nice they are, they won't like you anyway. I also really liked Gerry Cassidy. Gerry is universally respected in Washington for his political insights and wisdom. When I worked at the firm, it was run by Gerry and Jim Fabiani who later left to start his own government relations company. They were very nice people who genuinely believed in the cause of obtaining federal funds for universities and medical schools. They made my time in Washington a lot of fun. Jim once told me that my value to the company was more than as a rain maker. My affiliation with the firm stamped them as players in Washington. They were very good to me.

But I worked harder than I ever had in life at Cassidy,

wooing and landing clients, keeping those clients happy and finding new clients. It was an intensely busy time in my life because I not only had a demanding job but I also held the positions of Treasurer of the Democratic National Committee and Treasurer of the Democratic Governors Association.

At my office at Cassidy, I installed several phones with multiple lines. I engaged in an elaborate phone dance every day with staffers manning phones and flagging me to take calls, drop calls and switch calls. Joe Tarver, my chief of staff at Cassidy, placed calls for my Cassidy work. He sat on the sofa and faced me and then placed phone calls, one after the other, on a phone with four separate lines. He would put calls through, interrupt me with a hand signal or sometimes even a hand written sign, and make judgments about who could be put on hold and who needed to be put through immediately. Dan Cooney, my DNC staffer, did the same thing. There were times were all the lines lit up at once and Joe and Dan signaled me as I juggled calls, cajoling and convincing one after the other. Joe and Dan took copious notes and reminded me of details concerning each caller.

I rented a luxurious penthouse condominium in the Washington Harbor complex overlooking the Potomac River in the fashionable Georgetown section of Washington, D.C. I hired a butler, Miguel, a legal immigrant who paid all his taxes and filed all the appropriate paperwork including Social Security, to be home during the day. Someone had to be there to unlock the door for the caterer and keep the place clean. I entertained constantly. Hosting a breakfast, lunch, cocktail hour and dinner on the same day was not unusual. In my capacity as Treasurer of the Democratic National Committee, the chairman, Ron Brown, and I often invited donors from across the country to have dinner with at least six Senators in attendance, primarily those who were up for reelection in the next two years. In my capacity as Treasurer of the Democratic Governor's Association, whenever a Democratic governor came to Washington, I hosted a welcome event at the penthouse and the governor's office would typically invite the guests to include people with a connection to his or her home state.

Every day the caterers swept in, set up the event, served, cleaned up and then did it all over again. We would set up tables in the living room and have six Senators and 30 others and bring in big fundraisers from around the country. If the governor of North Dakota came to Washington, I'd host a reception of 50 people and invite people who had an interest in the state. Years afterwards, strangers would walk up to me and greet me like a long lost friend and recall a delightful evening at my condo. I have to confess that I met so many people and hosted so many events that I cannot remember many of these guests.

Joe Tarver was a native Texan and he remembers a fundraising dinner for 10 held for Ann Richards, then the state Treasurer in Texas, to help raise money for her campaign for governor. When Ann won that race, we stopped by to

THE MONEY GUY

pay a courtesy call when in Austin for Cassidy business. I sent her two dozen yellow roses and those roses were on her desk when we walked into the office. We enjoyed tea served by the governor herself.

I commuted from Brookline to Washington leaving Logan Airport in Boston on Monday morning and flying back from Reagan National on Friday morning, a congressional schedule. The distance, however, took a toll on my relationship with Tim McNeil. Tim fell in love with one of his closest friends and we broke up after 17 years. While the work was exhilarating and exhausting, the break up marked a very sad and painful time for me personally.

My waistline expanded with all of that rich food and drinking. I smoked cigarettes which helped me drop a few pounds but kept trying to quit smoking which made me short tempered and caused me to gain even more weight. One of the many times I tried to quit, Joe Tarver pleaded with me to keep smoking because my mood soured when I tried to quit.

But the next presidential campaign was hovering on the horizon. I always felt Bill Clinton, the governor of Arkansas, was one of the most persuasive speakers in the Democratic Party. I had met him through my work for the Democratic Governors Association. During the primary season in 1988, I was flying on the Dukakis campaign plane from Atlanta to Texas and someone suggested I be dropped off in Little Rock to talk to Bill Clinton and see if he would endorse Mike Dukakis. The private jet landed at the airport

THE RAINMAKER

and a state trooper picked me up and took me to the governor's mansion not far from downtown Little Rock. We had drinks and talked for several hours. I tried to convince him to endorse Dukakis. I thought we had a terrific time. The next day, Clinton endorsed Al Gore. I decided I better stick to fundraising and leave the politics to others.

But I pushed for Bill to be keynote speaker at the Democratic National Convention in Atlanta in 1988. A convention hall is a very difficult venue for speakers. His speech did not go over well. He always blamed the fact that the lights were not dimmed for his speech so the conventioneers kept on talking to one another instead of listening to him. Even though the speech seemed too long and he knew early on that he had lost the audience in the hall, he had a commitment to say certain nice things about Mike Dukakis to the national television audience so he soldiered on. When I got home to Brookline after the 1988 convention, I was exhausted from a nonstop week of speeches and meetings and the excitement of watching Dukakis accept the party nomination. The phone rang and it was Bill Clinton apologizing to me for the speech and explaining what happened. I got a second call that night from Jesse Jackson requesting his own plane for the general election campaign. Jackson stayed in the Democratic primary contest until the bitter end long after Dukakis wrapped up the nomination. Sasso sent me to Chicago with Kristin Demong to talk to Jackson after the convention. We were picked up by a huge limousine at the airport and driven to Jesse's house on the South Side of Chicago. Jackson had

THE MONEY GUY

arranged for us to have dinner at a restaurant in downtown Chicago at a round table right in the middle of the place where everyone could see us. Jackson pitched us hard on how effective he would be as a surrogate for Dukakis. He kept saying he was a team player and wanted to be in the huddle. I told him that Dukakis was a solitary long distance runner and there were no huddles in this campaign. We gave him what he wanted and he was so pleased to be able to fly around the country on his own plane that he did not create any more disruption for the rest of the campaign.

Despite the speech disaster, I always saw Clinton as a potential president. He had the right stuff. He was extremely intelligent, personable and a charismatic and engaging man. About a year after I moved to Washington, I met with Bill whom I met earlier through the Democratic Governors Association (Bill served as chairman of the DGA in 1986 and 1987) and Bruce Lindsey and told him that I wanted to work for him if he ran for President. But he made a pledge to the people of Arkansas to serve out his full term if reelected governor of Arkansas which took him out of contention for 1992. After he made that announcement, he called and released me from my pledge. At that point, Dick Gephardt, one of Dukakis' rivals in 1988, wanted to run for President again and he approached me when I was working at Cassidy. He came to see me at my office which was a very big deal. The Majority Leader of the U.S. House does not typically pay a call on a lobbyist in his office. He invited me to dinner with his wife Jane so we could get to know one another better. He asked me to be Treasurer of his campaign. Dick Gephardt is a superb person. He has the unusual ability to seem totally in command as he listens rather than talks. But Dick changed his mind after he commissioned a poll in New England that convinced him George H.W. Bush was unbeatable in 1992. The poll suggested Bush had the same Teflon coating as Ronald Reagan, a view reinforced by the surge of patriotism after the first Gulf War. That wave of patriotism convinced many pundits Bush was sitting pretty for 1992 but history shows that wave ebbed back out to sea.

About this time, I started to think about leaving Washington. I really liked the people at Cassidy & Associates but an old friend, Patrick J. McGovern, the owner of International Data Group (IDG), asked me if I would consider becoming vice chairman of IDG. He heads up the world's leading technology media, events and research company. He began his career in publishing when he was an undergraduate at MIT on the first computer magazine in the country. He got in on the ground floor of the computer industry and his company now oversees more than 300 magazines and newspapers and an online network of more than 450 web sites. Pat is one of the smartest men I have ever known. I was best man when he married Lore Harp, who is also an extraordinary entrepreneur, inventor and high tech pioneer. Lore says she thought I was full of myself when we first met but we subsequently became very good friends. Lore does not suffer fools and, more than once, she has taken me down a peg when I got too puffed up. To me, that is a sign of a genuine friend. I was

◄ **THE MONEY GUY**

flattered by Pat's offer and moved back to Boston when I accepted it.

After Gephardt decided against running, I resumed my talks with Bruce Lindsey, an Arkansas lawyer who was one of Bill Clinton's best friends. Bruce is a steady, quiet man of tremendous competence and sound judgment. He acted as consigliore to Clinton for years and served him loyally and well through some tough times. He eventually became president of the William J. Clinton Foundation. During that period of time, Al Gore approached me and asked me to get involved in his campaign but I was not ready to make a decision. I became close to Bruce Lindsey and told him that I felt very strongly Bill Clinton should run in 1992.

Clinton realized there was an opportunity for someone like him in 1992. He was closely aligned with the Democratic Leadership Council, a group of moderate Democrats who espoused a ``Third Way" that was not liberal or conservative but a pragmatic different more independent approach. In his book, ``*My Life*", Clinton says he realized that there was an opening for a DLC Democrat who could relate to the base of the party and swing voters. He took some soundings as he traveled around the country for the DLC and then traveled around his home state asking his constituents if they thought he should run for President in 1992. He got enough encouragement so by the late summer of 1992, he created an exploratory committee and in September, I called a press conference in Washington and announced my resignation as treasurer of the Democratic

THE RAINMAKER

National Committee so I could go to Little Rock and become treasurer of Bill Clinton's presidential campaign.

When I arrived in Little Rock, I spoke to about 200 people in a ballroom. Clinton had not announced he was running for President so I gave a speech saying he should run. I remember saying that if he ran, Little Rock would never be the same. Arkansas is not a wealthy state by any estimation but I told the Clinton team he had to raise $1 million in his home state. Mack McLarty, the prominent Arkansas businessman who, like Clinton, was born in Hope, Arkansas and was in the same kindergarten class as Bill, became the finance chair in Arkansas. At the time, McLarty was the chairman and CEO of Arkla, the huge natural gas company. We became great friends. In his book, Bill Clinton recalls that he was able to raise early money partially because of me. He wrote of me that ``regular Democratic donors ... would give just because (Bob Farmer) asked them''. It was true. Not too many people thought he had much of a chance back then. Bill called Pat and Lore McGovern one morning about 5:30 a.m. (He miscalculated the time difference) to apologize for taking me away from IDG. Lore always said that my asking Bill to make that phone call was ``classic Bob.''

Living back in Boston, I hosted my first political event since returning to the state fulltime for Bill Clinton. Bill and Hillary flew in for it and stayed at my house in Brookline. I never worked harder on an event. No one in Massachusetts really knew much about Clinton other than

THE MONEY GUY

he was governor of Arkansas and he delivered a bad speech at Dukakis' nominating convention in Atlanta. I begged people to give me $250 and $500 for that first event. There was a lot of pressure on me because I had a reputation to hold up as a major fundraiser and if I could not deliver for my candidate in my home state, something was very wrong. So I went to my friends and said, ``You and I have been friends for a long time and I will always be there for you. I have Bill Clinton coming to my home and you can't let me be embarrassed in my own home.'' My friends came through for me and I raised $80,000 but it was the hardest $80,000 I ever raised. I took Bill and Hillary to dinner one night at the Brae Burn Country Club and I remember Bill and Bob Reich, the Kennedy School professor who later became Secretary of Labor in the Clinton administration, sat in the parking lot and talked policy for half an hour. It seemed like hours as I waited for them to finish their policy talk.

Tim and I moved out of the Master Bedroom so Bill and Hillary could take the room. People have been analyzing their relationship for years but I was struck by how devoted they were to one another and how connected they were to their only child, Chelsea who was then a little girl of 11. Hillary's parents ended up moving into the governor's mansion to provide stability for Chelsea during the campaign but both Bill and Hillary kept in close touch with their daughter. Each got on the kitchen phone to talk to her about her homework when they stayed with me.

THE RAINMAKER

The Dalai Lama had been a house guest some time before because of Tim's work as his American publisher. The Dalai Lama is literally considered a god in Tibet and when we drove out to one of his lectures, about 150 Tibetans lined our long driveway with their foreheads touched to the ground in his honor. It was an extraordinary scene. I remember telling Bill Clinton about this and adding, ``If you are lucky, you may change your first name to Mr. President but you will never be a god,'' like his holiness the Dalai Lama.

I convinced another friend of mine, Axel Leblois, an accomplished Frenchman who was then president of Bull HN Worldwide Information Systems, to host a fundraiser for Clinton at his home in Wellesley. I assigned two volunteers to help him and they approached the vice presidents of the firm who were responsible for contracts and purchasing. We convinced all the company suppliers to show up. In truth, a lot of Republicans attended the event but it was a terrific evening. And Clinton remembered. Years later when I was serving in Bermuda, I got a call from the White House and they said the President wants to know the name of that Frenchman who hosted the event for him in Boston. The Clinton's were planning a State Dinner for the President of France. He invited Axel and his wife to that dinner. Axel never asked him for a thing but I give the President a lot of credit for remembering someone who helped him early.

For Clinton, I reached out to my fundraising friends from

THE MONEY GUY

the Dukakis campaign. When I called Clay Constantinou in New Jersey, Clay felt a bit conflicted because he felt an obligation to help former Senator Paul E. Tsongas of Massachusetts who was also Greek-American. But I told him Bill Clinton was going to win and Clay would be the finance chairman for New Jersey. Clay raised $4 million for Clinton in New Jersey and the local newspapers called him ``Clinton's $4 million Man in New Jersey''. The grateful President later named Clay US Ambassador to Luxembourg.

David Wilhelm, a gifted campaign operative from Chicago, was Clinton's campaign manager. He wanted to hire a young aggressive guy from Chicago to be the campaign finance director. He flew Rahm Emanuel to Brookline to meet me. I was impressed and we hired him. From day one, it was not much fun because Rahm was as competitive as Kristin Demong, my finance director on the Dukakis' campaign, had been supportive. Rahm uses a lot of salty language. He screamed and yelled and frightened people into submission. I am much more low key. Rahm was very effective but that type of style takes a real toll on relationships. I always admired Rahm for his total loyalty to Bill Clinton in good times and in bad. You want Rahm on your side during a fight. Years later Rahm served in the White House as a senior aide to Clinton before running for Congress from his home town of Chicago. He left the congressional seat to serve as Barack Obama's chief of staff and then returned home to run for mayor of Chicago.

THE RAINMAKER

During that campaign I traveled around the country. I quickly realized this campaign was different from the Dukakis campaign. The Philadelphia Inquirer did a full page article on me when I was raising money for Bill in Pennsylvania. The campaign press staff was very upset with me even though it was a very positive piece for both me and the campaign. The press staff was very territorial.

My teammates on this campaign were Vic Raiser, the lawyer and Democratic fundraiser, and Ken Brody, a Goldman Sachs executive who later became chairman of the Export-Import Bank during the Clinton administration. Vic and his wife Molly became very good friends. Vic tragically died in a plane crash on July 30, 1992 while on a fly fishing trip in Alaska with his son Monty and some of Monty's friends. Monty had just graduated from Princeton, Vic's alma mater. It was a huge loss and I miss Vic and his friendship to this day. Clinton made Molly chief of Protocol. She is a lovely woman and I treasure her friendship.

Vic was in charge of our fundraising in Washington, D.C. All fundraisers are competitive and during the Democratic National Convention in New York City, we were all at the Americana Hotel on 7th Avenue. I held meetings with prominent fundraisers in my suite. Governor Clinton had a suite on a higher floor. One afternoon I got a call from Vic. He said that he was with Governor Clinton going over the convention speech. He asked if I would like to come up to Clinton's suite.

Face time with the candidate is always at a premium. I

◄ THE MONEY GUY

didn't understand why Vic would be invited to review the Governor's speech but I was only too happy to join them.

``I'll be right up,'' I said.

``Never mind,'' said Vic, ``I was just kidding.'' That was one of the best practical jokes of the campaign.

The Clinton campaign had a rule that no fundraisers were allowed on his campaign plane. As Treasurer, I was the exception. I never moved to Little Rock. I traveled a lot and was at a time in my life where I really did not want to make Little Rock my base of operation. The younger people on the campaign who were based in Little Rock benefited from being at headquarters all the time and could play internal politics, sometimes at my expense.

On election night in Little Rock, I welcomed all of the people who had raised money for Clinton's campaign. It was very exciting to finally have a winner and I discovered election night is a lot more fun when you win the presidency. The night now is a blur. Everyone was hugging everyone else. We were so elated. Not only were we personally delighted to see positive results from all our hard work but we were thrilled at the prospects of a Democrat and a friend living at 1600 Pennsylvania Avenue.

A month later, Clinton threw a party to thank all the major fundraisers at the most elegant downtown hotel in Little

THE RAINMAKER

Rock. I sat at the last table and I was the last person he greeted. When he got to me, he gave me a big hug. It was one of the proudest moments of my life.

The day after the election, I asked Mack McLarty if I could visit with the President-Elect. I arrived at the governor's mansion for an 8:30 a.m. meeting and was sitting in the reception area. Three men arrived and two had handcuffs holding their briefcases to their wrists. They were from the CIA and came to brief the President-Elect. The third man was R. James Woolsey whom Clinton would name CIA director the next month. Imagine how I felt when the Governor's Secretary came in and said, ``The President-Elect will see Mr. Farmer next."

He was incredibly gracious as always. I had a list of people who had worked hard for him to review with him as he considered appointments. The first name I mentioned was Madeleine Albright. He said, ``I've already offered her Ambassador to the United Nations and she is coming here with her two daughters for the announcement."

During the next few weeks, a list of White House aides was announced. I was a little disappointed that no one had even called me and expressed that disappointment to John Sasso who called Eli Segal, a Massachusetts businessman who was a senior adviser to Clinton. The next day, Eli called and asked me to serve as Treasurer of the Inauguration. Needless to say, I was pleased to be asked so I moved back to Washington and lived in a hotel at government expense with a car and military driver. We raised a ton of money for

◄ **THE MONEY GUY**

the inauguration because corporations can give unlimited amounts and they all want to impress the new president.

Although a lot of people were lining up to take jobs in the Clinton administration, I was reluctant. I was painfully aware of the firestorm that erupted when Clinton nominated Roberta Achtenberg, a lesbian who was a San Francisco Supervisor, to the administration as an assistant secretary at the Department of Housing and Urban Development. Jesse Helms, the conservative Senator from North Carolina, denounced her as a ``militant extremist''. Most of the top jobs in Washington need Senate approval and I did not want to risk a public denouncement for being gay.

After Clinton took office, I brought my brother and sister in law to a dinner for Democratic Governors. My sister in law wanted to meet the President and asked me to join her in the rope line. I felt a little silly because I knew Bill Clinton very well but I agreed to do it for Jackie. We were the last in line and when Clinton spotted me, he threw his arms around me and said, ``Bob, call this number. I want to see you in the Oval Office tomorrow morning.'' My sister-in-law was quite delighted by that. So was I.

The next day I went to the White House. I thought a lot about what I wanted to say. I said, ``Mr. President, I've given this a lot of thought. If you nominate me for something, I might be confirmed but it will be unpleasant for me and my family and take up a lot of your political capital. So I will take a job outside of the administration.'' I think Clinton was relieved. And I took a job with GE Alstom, a

THE RAINMAKER

French company that built high speed rail and wanted to build a rail line between Dallas and Houston. I discovered early on that Clinton was serious about balancing the federal budget which meant that the federal government was not going to be giving Texas $8 billion to build a high speed rail line so after a few months, I told the company that I didn't want them to waste their money any longer and I resigned.

I went back to Florida but I felt bad. Everyone I knew from the Clinton campaign seemed to be working for the government and part of this wonderful new administration. The beginning of a new presidency is a heady, exhilarating time when optimism reigns and everything seems possible. I felt left out. I made an appointment to see Bruce Lindsey who was one of the President's closest friends and top aides. I told him I didn't want to ask for an ambassadorship but I would like to be involved somehow so I suggested going on the board of Fannie Mae, the housing giant. But then my good friend John Sasso said he wanted to be on the board. So I said give it to him. Then they offered me a slot on the Amtrak Board of Directors and I met with the Secretary of Transportation to discuss it.

But fortune intervened. Three friends from the Clinton campaign: Craig Smith, Mark Middleton, and Matt Gorman, were having lunch together in Washington and they realized that I had not been named to anything. They came up with the idea of US Consul to Bermuda. I had helped all three of them. I recommended Craig for the

THE MONEY GUY

job of finance director of the campaign because he had been in charge of state boards and commissions during Clinton's time as governor. I had helped Mark after he had a run in with Hillary Clinton. I smoothed things over and saved his job as finance director for the state of Arkansas. And Matt had been a waiter at Paolo's, a restaurant in Georgetown for two years who told me he wanted to learn how to fundraise when I worked at Cassidy. At first, I had no idea how to use Matt. I could not sell him to a client. He had never worked on Capitol Hill or for a corporation. I advised him to get a job as a congressional aide and get some experience and stay in touch. At the time, Matt was 29, as he turned to go. He told me, ``When I was a kid, I wanted to be John F. Kennedy. When I was a teenager, I wanted to be Hugh Hefner. Now I want to be the next Bob Farmer.'' No one had ever said that to me. I took a second look at him and thought about it. He had graduated from Georgetown University and he was clearly smart. He had a lot of energy and a terrific attitude. I decided to give him a chance and brought him to Boston with me, invited him to stay in my house and raise money for John Silber, the former President of Boston University who had just won the Democratic gubernatorial nomination. Matt ran out and bought himself a business suit the day I gave him the job. His mother hemmed the pants and he drove up to Brookline the next day. Silber lost but it had nothing to do with money. Matt did a great job and has been part of my team ever since. He came to Little Rock with me when I joined the Clinton campaign and became a masterful logistical genius in the finance operation. Matt often says that my secret is getting people to still like me after I take a crow bar to their wallets.

So all three felt an allegiance to me. Each had a top job in the administration. Craig was White House Political Director; Mark was the deputy to the President's Chief of Staff; Matt was a liaison between the Treasury Department and White House, a job that he initially found disappointing. Matt wanted to work in the West Wing. When he called me to express his disappointment, I told him he was nuts. Working in the West Wing is terrible. Everyone is uptight about his own career and completely paranoid about position and status. I told him he should be grateful he would be meeting every major CEO in America. He soon came to recognize the wisdom of my opinion.

During a meeting to discuss ambassadorial appointments, my friends recommended me for the Bermuda job but Vice President Al Gore's chief of staff said Gore had a candidate for that job. But Gore's staffer said I deserved it more so my name went to the President. However, Clinton put a question mark next to it with a note ``let's discuss.''

I learned this right away because I had so many friends working in the West Wing. I was afraid the President would withhold his approval because he thought I was not interested based on our earlier conversation. So I called Katie Whelan whom I had worked with at the Democratic Governors Association and told her that I had to talk to the President. She invited me to an upcoming DGA golf tournament in Indiana that the President was scheduled to

◄ THE MONEY GUY

attend. She made sure I got close to the President. I have a photograph of President Clinton, then-Governor Evan Bayh (He later became a US Senator from Indiana, the job his father, Birch Bayh once held) and me from that day. In that picture, I am saying, ``Mr. President, I understand my name has come up for the job of US Consul in Bermuda. I want you to know that I would be honored and privileged to do that job.''

Not long afterwards, I was in Boston playing gin with eight of my pals. I noticed a message on my cell phone. It was Craig Smith calling from the White House. ``Bob,'' he said. ``I wanted to be the first to congratulate you. President Clinton signed the papers to name you the U.S. consul General in Bermuda.'' I played the message for my card playing buddies and they burst into applause.

It did not escape me that I got this amazing plum job representing my country on an exquisite island because of the young people I had helped in the past. I have always believed in sharing the credit and nurturing talented people. Seeing that investment paid back in such an incredible way was an affirmation to me of my style and modus operandi. I was off to Bermuda for the next adventure in my life.

CHAPTER 7

Living in Paradise

The U.S. Consul General to Bermuda, like only two others, those in Hong Kong and Jerusalem, reports directly to the Secretary of State, just like a U.S. Ambassador. While the position does not warrant a formal public hearing, it does require Senate confirmation. My first obstacle popped up in the U.S. Senate when Senator Claiborne Pell, the powerful chairman of the Senate Foreign Relations Committee, objected to my appointment.

Pell was a member of the New England aristocracy, a quirky old school Yankee Brahmin who jogged in a tweed coat and assigned a staff person to the issue of extrasensory perception (ESP), one of his passions. He served six full terms as the U.S. Senator from the tiny state of Rhode Island and despite his WASP pedigree was beloved by a blue collar constituency until his death at the age of 90 on January 1, 2009. Pell had no particular objection to me but he had served as a Foreign Service officer early in his career and he was philosophically opposed to political

◄ THE MONEY GUY

appointments for certain foreign postings, including the job of U.S. Consul General to Bermuda.

The job had traditionally been a Foreign Service posting until the beginning of Ronald Reagan's first term in 1981 when Max Friedersdorf, a friend and campaign supporter of Reagan, asked for the job and the President, not knowing it was a career slot reserved for a Foreign Service Officer, readily agreed. When the President makes a decision that is it. The buck really stops on his desk. Since then, the job had become a much envied patronage position despite Pell's objections.

But Pell's concerns could not be ignored by the new Democratic President. As the Senate Foreign Relations Committee Chairman Pell was the single most influential lawmaker on issues affecting the U.S. State Department and the Clinton administration needed Pell on its side.

Senator Pell knew me and my work for the Democratic National Committee so he called me personally at the Watergate Hotel where I was staying to tell me that he had no quarrel with me personally and admired the contributions I made to the Democratic Party and would support me for a major ambassadorial appointment. But he had been strongly against the Bermuda job being political ever since President Reagan made the first political appointment and just felt he needed to remain consistent and insist it be a Foreign Service appointment. Foreign Service Officers are the highly skilled professional diplomats who make a career formulating and implementing the foreign policy of the United States. I appreciated the phone call but I wanted the job so I got off the phone and called Wendy Sherman, a brilliant woman who was then the assistant Secretary for Legislative Affairs at the State Department. Wendy had a tremendous career including a stint as President and CEO of the Fanny Mae Foundation and eventually became Counselor of the Department of State, a position that held the rank of ambassador. She is now a principal in former Secretary of State Madeleine Albright's consulting firm in Washington.

During the dustup over Roberta Achtenberg's appointment, Pell went to the Senate floor to defend Achtenberg and revealed that his daughter Julia L.W. Pell was a lesbian. Pell took the conservative challenge to Achtenberg personally and said he would not want his daughter denied an opportunity to serve her country simply because of her sexual orientation.

Wendy is not only smart on policy but she has a lot of political smarts, too. She went directly to Pell and explained that I was being named to this job in part because I was gay and wanted to avoid being exposed and excoriated in public by Senator Jesse Helms of North Carolina and other conservatives as Achtenberg had been. Pell was a very kind and decent man and he withdrew his opposition and let my appointment go through without comment. His daughter Julie helped get a gay rights law passed in Rhode Island and sadly died of lung cancer in 2006.

So I slipped in under the radar. Kirk O'Donnell, a talented

◀ THE MONEY GUY

Boston political operative who was counsel to House Speaker Tip O'Neill, told me to never feel short changed because he believed I received one of the plum jobs in government. Some appointments may have been more glamorous or prestigious but nothing beat Bermuda for lifestyle. Indeed, the Washington Post described the job as ``the softest, cushiest, most delightful job in the U.S. Government." I would never argue with the Post on that point.

I attended ambassador training school which is known as ``charm school", an intense two week briefing for ambassadors and chiefs of mission, with 15 other appointees and learned how to run an embassy. During that training session, we were taken in a plane without windows to the home of the Army's Delta Force in North Carolina and had a day of training with the Delta Force to prepare us for terrorist attacks. Before we went, the State Department made us sign a confidentiality document pledging to keep secret anything we saw on the base. I was surprised when I later read the paperback book ``Delta Force", a bestselling book on the Army's counterterrorism force that anyone could pick up at any airport which pretty much included everything we learned that day.

Some of the ambassador designates were assigned to hot spots and could not take their families with them. Bermuda was not one of those assignments. At charm school, one of the suggestions they made was to make sure I set out framed photographs of myself with powerful friends, such as the President and members of the Senate, in the new overseas office and home. Evidently, that sort of proof of friendship helps build the credibility of an envoy.

Afterwards, I went to Boston to visit my good friend Ron Ansin and Ron woke me up about 11 p.m. one night with a call from the State Department. It was official. My appointment did not require a Senate hearing but it was among the routine appointments that go to the Senate for a perfunctory unanimous consent approval en bloc on a long list of military promotions and Foreign Service appointments.

I flew to Washington the next day and Mark Weiner, a prominent Democratic fundraiser from Rhode Island who made his fortune selling political paraphernalia and a good friend, witnessed a hurried oath taking ceremony by a clerk at the State Department. Several months later I came back for a public swearing in ceremony in the beautiful diplomatic reception rooms at the State Department. The rooms are furnished with a spectacular collection of 18th century American antique furniture, paintings and decorative arts. Vice President Al Gore agreed to swear me in despite a foot injury. He was hobbling around on crutches because of a ruptured Achilles tendon. Tim Wirth, the former Senator from Colorado and the first Undersecretary for Global Affairs, acted as the master of ceremonies. My dear friend Molly Raiser had been named Chief of Protocol by President Bill Clinton so she graciously introduced everyone. My brothers and their wives and all my nieces, nephews and cousins and hundreds of friends attended

THE MONEY GUY

as well as a number of Democratic senators including Ted Kennedy, John Glenn, John Kerry, Evan Bayh and Howard Metzenbaum. Molly said it was the largest reception she had ever seen. It was quite a euphoric feeling to take the oath of office as the U.S. Consul General and know I was now representing the President and the United States of America in Bermuda as my adopted son Thieu held the Farmer family Bible. Afterwards, I hosted a dinner at Union Station for the out of town guests that turned into quite a roast of me.

Bermuda is a glorious place, a British territory located just 640 miles off the coast of Cape Hatteras, North Carolina in the North Atlantic. The weather is just about perfect. In the summer the temperature ranges between 70 and 85 degrees and in the winter it hovers at a pleasant 70 degrees, cool enough to toss on a light jacket when you head out to the links. The island is actually 181 separate islands. The largest is Main Island and Main Island is what is commonly called Bermuda. The islands take up less than 21 square miles but include seven championship golf courses. Bermuda has long been a favorite destination for honeymooners. In fact, Bill and Hillary Clinton spent their honeymoon there. Tourism and insurance are the big industries but fun is really what Bermuda is all about. It is a delightful place of graceful living.

A benefit of this posting was the official residence of the U.S. Consul, a magnificent classic Bermuda style mansion on the south coast of the island called Chelston. Chelston was built in 1941 by C.P. Dubbs, the son of Jesse Dubbs who developed a process of cracking crude oil which breaks it down into its component parts to make new petroleum products including petroleum jelly. This was the basis of Jesse Dubbs' fortune and the reason he named his son Carbon Petroleum Dubbs, affectionately referred to as C.P. Lest we feel too sorry for C.P. being saddled with this unusual name, he liked it enough that he named his son Carbon Petroleum Dubbs Jr.

C.P. also made a fortune in oil and a chair in chemical engineering carries his name at the Massachusetts Institute of Technology in Cambridge. C.P. lived at Chelston until his death in 1962 at the age of 81. His heirs deeded the estate to the United States government in 1964 to settle a tax debt. The house is located on 14 acres overlooking the ocean in Paget Parish. The mansion is 10,000 square feet with four bedrooms and fabulous public spaces suitable for entertaining dozens and dozens of guests. My father visited me there when he was 93 years old. We were sitting on the veranda surveying the glorious property one day, and Dad said, ``Bob, may I ask you a personal question?'' I said, ``Go ahead.''

Dad said, ``This is a beautiful piece of property. Do you plan to keep it or sell it?''

I told him, ``Dad, I'm just a steward here. It is the property of the United States Government.'' He said, ``Oh, it's part of your remuneration.'' I was always tickled that he was sharp enough to correctly use the word ``remuneration'' at his advanced age.

◄ **THE MONEY GUY**

The house has some unusual attributes. C.P. acquired rare wallpaper from a James River plantation house in Virginia and had it backed with canvas and moved to Chelston. The elaborate wallpaper featuring birds, insects and butterflies was reportedly hand painted by Chinese artists in London in the 17th century for a British tea merchant. The estate includes: a guest house; grape vines; an orchard of fruit trees including fig, orange, apple, pear, peach, loquat, guava, Surinam cherry and mulberry; a 200 foot long private sandy beach and a beach house on a prime spot on Grape Bay. It cost about $300,000 a year to maintain it but in my view it was worth every penny.

When I flew to Bermuda, I was greeted by Eddie Foggo, a former police lieutenant and my chauffeur. Eddie and I became fast friends. He helped me enormously with his extensive knowledge of local lore and his understanding of protocol. Years later, I was pleased to attend his wedding in Boston. I sailed through customs with my new diplomatic passport and Eddie drove me to the residence.

I was stunned when I first laid eyes on the house. I walked the grounds and made a call to the Mid Ocean Golf Club to make a tee time for the next morning. My position made me an honorary member of all the golf and yacht clubs in Bermuda. In fact, Bill Clinton always said that he sent me to ``golf school'' for five years. I did not know anyone in Bermuda yet so I called Joel and Sally Montgomery in Miami.

``You won't believe this place,'' I told them, ``you have to come over right away.''

LIVING IN PARADISE

Just then the doorbell rang.

``Who was at the door?'' asked Joel.

``Well, that was the pizza man,'' I replied.

``Where is the cook?'' he asked.

``On vacation for two weeks,'' I said.

``We'll see you in two weeks,'' said Joel.

While the federal government covers the overhead cost of an official residence, the expense of entertaining falls upon the ambassadors. I hosted between 6 and 10 guests a week at Chelston during the five years I served as Consul and entertained constantly. It was a huge personal delight for me to host everyone important in my life dating back to grade and high school, college and law school. All my relatives visited, some more than once. Most of my friends, including Dellson Alberts who works on the business side of the Boston Globe, made it to the island at least once. Some came more often. During my first month there, my brother, Brent, visited. One day, we were walking together on the beach and he asked: ``Would it be lacking in family affection if I only visit you once a month?''

I opened the mansion up to the people of Bermuda and used it to develop good will for the United States and for U.S. business. I also somehow managed to lose 32 pounds because Maria DeSilva, the cook who worked at Chelston, kept me on a diet and made sure I ate healthy low fat food. It was an unexpected bonus from my service to finally get my weight down. I told everyone it was probably my biggest achievement.

The government sold Chelston to a wealthy hedge fund owner in 2000 because Congress decided these beautiful overseas properties were costing the government too much money. I thought it was a penny wise pound foolish decision. The U.S. government still has the obligation to house the U.S. Consul so there really are not any savings for giving up a property it owned outright. But the image of a public servant living in such splendor made for great sensational television pictures.

Andrea Mitchell of NBC News did a story on *The Fleecing of America* that featured Chelston among other properties. I knew the story was coming and called John Sasso to ask for advice. John told me not to comment because we all knew it would be a negative story. If you know a reporter is doing a negative story, it's a bad idea to grant an interview because in the context of a 30 minute interview something you say will be taken out of context and be used to make you look really bad. The story included video taken from a helicopter panning the 14 acre grounds and went on and on about how cushy the job was. I called John after the newscast. He said, ``This is a very serious and very negative story.'' I responded, ``Didn't Chelston look great! Did you see the picture of me with Clinton in the Oval Office?''

He was thinking damage control while I was hoping all my

friends saw the piece. He told that story at my 60th birthday party and my friends all howled with laughter.

One of the benefits of having a friend in the White House is the opportunity to ride on Air Force One, the official jet of the President of the United States. President Clinton invited me to ride back to Washington from an event in Massachusetts. The blue and white jet with United States of America painted on the side is an iconic image. But the jet itself, a specially configured highly customized Boeing 747, lives up to the reputation. The front of the airplane includes a suite for the President with a bedroom, bathroom with shower, a study and a conference room. There are two galleys capable of serving 100 meals at a time. The plane has 87 telephone lines, video teleconferencing and big first class-sized leather seats for everyone.

I sat in the guest area in one of those oversized chairs next to Rep. J. Joseph Moakley, the delightful Democratic Congressman from South Boston who was chairman of the powerful Rules Committee. Joe Moakley was a charming and funny guy but I turned to him and said, ``Congressman, to most people talking to the chairman of the Rules Committee for two hours is a big deal. But I'm of the school that I would rather talk to my friends on the phone and tell them where I am." So I did. Each seat had an unsecure telephone. When you want to make a call from either the White House or Air Force One, you pick up the phone and tell them who you want to talk to. They place the telephone call and say, ``This is the White House

◄ **THE MONEY GUY**

Switchboard calling. Are you available to take a call from Mr. Farmer on Air Force One?" I told the operator to be sure and leave a message if she got voice mail.

I don't know if my friends got a kick out of that but I certainly did. I spent the entire flight on the telephone.

I was invited to several dinners at the White House as well. I took my former partner, Tim McNeill to one because it is a very special evening and I felt he deserved the experience of walking into that beautiful building escorted by the Marine Corps guards. Everything is flawless at a White House dinner from the presentation of the food to the flowers to the entertainment. The other guests are always interesting and it is always a huge honor to be a guest of the President of the United States and First Lady.

While living in Bermuda, I received an invitation from the White House to a state dinner for the President of Greece. I had two sisters-in-law and if I invited one, I'd be in big trouble with the other. So I called my best friend, Joel Montgomery in Florida and asked if he would mind if I invited his beautiful and gracious wife Sally to a dinner party without him. He said, ``I don't know why she would want to go but she is right here and you can ask her." I then asked Sally if she would like to go to a black tie state dinner at the White House. She could not say yes fast enough.

I flew in from Bermuda and they flew up from Miami and we all stayed at the Watergate Hotel. I arranged for a limo to take me and Sally to the White House. A few hours before the dinner, I was at the State Department for a briefing and I was told to call the White House Social Secretary. She said, ``Mr. Farmer, the President and Mrs. Clinton were wondering if you would like to spend the night at the White House?'' Of course, I accepted the invitation and then called Joel and said, ``Joel, this thing has escalated a little bit. Do you have a problem if Sally spends the night with me at the White House?''

He said, ``Yes!''

I said, ``Who don't you trust, Sally or me?''

He growled, ``I don't trust either of you!''

We found a solution. My friend Clay Constantinou who was then Ambassador to Luxembourg was also invited to the dinner. He agreed to escort Sally back to the Watergate Hotel and I stayed overnight in a guest room at the White House.

Mike and Kitty Dukakis were also invited to that dinner. Kitty and I were smokers so we went outside periodically to smoke. Every time we passed the Marine Corps guards to go outside, they snapped to attention. When we came back inside, they snapped to attention again. Later on when I retired to the guest room, the steward told me there was a coffee can on the roof for visiting smokers so I went up to the White House roof to smoke that night, found that coffee can and used it as an ashtray.

THE MONEY GUY

On another occasion, I took my son Thieu, to the white House to watch a movie with the President. It was a film about Iraq. Afterwards I remember Bill Clinton spent 45 minutes talking about the history of Iraq and the rivalries between its various ethnic groups. It was in the late 1990's, years before 9/11. To me it was one more demonstration of how bright and knowledgeable he is.

I had a great time in Bermuda. After breakfast, my driver would take me to the American Consulate to review official papers and deal with the business part of the job. Despite its reputation as a tourist destination, the location of the island also leads to drug smuggling and, in one case, an episode involving an attempt to smuggle a boat load of Chinese into the United States. The boat was diverted to Bermuda to keep it from landing on U.S. soil. Every time a representative from a federal agency, such as the Internal Revenue Service or the CIA, came to the island on official business, he or she had to check in with me as the senior U.S. official in Bermuda.

Half a million American tourists come to Bermuda each year so there is always some emergency involving a honeymooner who crashes a scooter or an issue involving the U.S. Naval base on the island. There were 2,300 military service people stationed at Naval Air Station Bermuda and they had families and dependents with them so the American military presence had a big economic impact on the island. The base closed during my time there and I was heavily involved in the extensive negotiations around its closing between the Department of Defense and the government of Bermuda. In fact, I took the premier in to the Oval Office for a courtesy call to President Clinton during that period of time. I loved the PX at the base and really missed it after the base closed. Because I entertained so much, I saved a lot of money shopping there.

I introduced some new traditions. I visited the prison every year and interviewed all of the American prisoners to make sure they were being treated properly. Most were incarcerated for drug offenses.

I threw a huge Fourth of July Party with fireworks each year at Chelston which was a big hit. Each year more than 3,000 people attended. Although U.S. foreign officials are not allowed to raise money, the one exception is the Fourth of July party. I went to all the big companies with American ties and asked for a $5,000 contribution. I raised more than $100,000 every year and asked each company to invite guests with American connections. I also invited other Americans. We offered rides for the kids, bands, food and drink. It was a wonderful way to celebrate America's birthday and brought the community together in a joyous way. No one had ever done that before.

The political officer at the Consulate kept track of outstanding achievements by individuals in Bermuda for me and I sent each a letter of congratulations on behalf of the American people. People told me those letters were very popular and ended up being posted on refrigerator doors and saved with other valued mementoes. I hosted a series

THE MONEY GUY

of breakfasts each week for various constituency groups including labor leaders, educators, and others at Chelston. Most of them had never set foot on the estate and they personally enjoyed seeing the magnificent property.

I met a lovely elderly woman, Ruth Rawlings Mott, the widow of Charles Stewart Mott, the largest single shareholder and a founder of General Motors. She invited me to tea at her beautiful home. So I decided I should reciprocate. I held a tea at Chelston for everyone on Bermuda who was over the age of 90. We identified them through churches and social organizations. About 25 to 30 people came, some with nurses and attendants in wheelchairs and with walkers and canes. They were pretty frail. The tea was scheduled for 4:30 p.m. At about 5:30, I said, ``I think I'll have a glass of wine'' and went to the bar. I nearly got crushed to death in the rush. Everyone wanted a drink! Tea did not quite make it.

I issued an open invitation to all of the White House staff to visit. White House staffers do not earn a lot of money and Bermuda is a quick flight for them. So I thought it would be a nice break for them. It was particularly fun for me because I got to hear all the gossip from Washington. A few took me up on it including Bruce Lindsey and Cheryl Mills, Betty Curry, the President's personal secretary, and Nancy Heinreich, the deputy assistant for appointments and scheduling and Stephanie Street, the President's scheduler. My friends in the White House reciprocated by arranging private tours of the White House for my friends.

LIVING IN PARADISE ➤

I did a lot of public speaking to different groups while I was in Bermuda because many organizations and companies hold meetings and conventions there. I golfed four or five times a week and my handicap improved quite a bit. I took a swim about a half a mile out to the reef every day. It was idyllic.

Captain Tim Bryan, the charismatic and talented head of the Naval Station, and I golfed with the governor and his number two man every week. The governor was not a very good golfer but we enjoyed one another's company. Despite the caliber of the golf, this weekly outing provided us the opportunity to share information and views in a relaxed social setting.

One evening I attended a very formal dinner and was seated with the Premier, Sir John Swan. At the next table were Ross Perot and his wife Margot who had a home in Bermuda. Each table sat eight. Two of the guests who were supposed to be seated with the Perot's did not show up and the host approached the Premier and asked if he and his wife would like to move to the Perot's table. Sir John didn't miss a beat, but said, `We're very happy with the folks we're with now." I was impressed by his courtesy and lack of pretension.

Another time, Lord Waddington, the Governor, hosted a dinner at Government House, the largest mansion in Bermuda and the official residence of the British Governor on the occasion of a NATO fleet visit. Admirals and captains of the fleet attended the dinner along with a few local dignitaries. After the usual round of speeches and toasts... it was a very elegant dinner...I was struck by the fact that it seemed that all the attendees were like actors on the stage. Each of us played our parts for a prescribed period of time, and recited our lines. We held these jobs for two or three years and each of us would be replaced fairly shortly. It was a somewhat sobering thought. Sic transit Gloria.

One day I got a call from the Minister of Finance, who owned a beautiful home on the ocean. He reported that a World War II era bomb had washed up on his beach. A US Naval aircraft carrier was anchored off the shore of Bermuda and he asked if the Navy could retrieve the bomb. So I contacted the officer in charge and asked if he could remove the bomb safely. The officer said that was not something the Navy did.

But I had an ace in the hole. My friend John Dalton, the Secretary of the Navy, invited me and a friend or two to attend the annual Army Navy football game each year. Dalton, an investment banker from Texas, was one of our key fundraisers in the Lone Star State in 1992. The Army-Navy invitation was much coveted. Dalton and the Secretary of the Army invited all of the admirals and generals to travel to the game on a reserved train from Union Station in Washington, D.C. The train featured food, drinks and a carnival-like atmosphere. Special busses carried us to the playing field in a motorcade and we sat in a special reserved section of the field. When the President of

LIVING IN PARADISE ➤

the United States attended the game, he would sit on the Navy side for half the game and then switch and sit on the Army side for the second half. In fact, one year Bill Clinton spotted me at the game and called out, ``That was a good meeting we had yesterday, Bob.'' The flag officers looked very impressed and my stature rose in their eyes. What they did not know is that Clinton and I had spent five minutes in the Oval Office gossiping about mutual friends and current events.

So when the officer indicated he could not help me, I said, ``By the way, did I meet you on the train to the Army-Navy game?'' He seemed very surprised. ``Were you on the train?'' he asked. I said, ``My good friend is John Dalton, the Secretary of the Navy. If you can't help me, I guess I will have to call him.'' After a very pregnant pause, he said, ``We'll take care of it tomorrow.''

I always loved attending those games with the high ranking military officials because I never rose above an E2 when I served in the Army Reserve.

It helps to have friends in high places

Official Bermuda is very British and formal. A typical invitation would invite guests to show up at 7 p.m. and it would also say the Governor, Lord Waddington, and his wife will arrive at 7:15 p.m. Protocol called for everyone to arrive before the Governor and to stay until he left. It was rude to show up late or leave early. I remember some guests sidling up me at Chelston and begging me

◄ **THE MONEY GUY**

to convince the Governor to go home if a dinner ran late because they could not leave until he did.

Bermuda was so formal I had to buy a formal grey flannel morning suit with a top hat and vest and coat that came down to my knees. I wore it a lot. Every year the governor hosted a party to celebrate the birthday of the Queen of England and I represented the United States at the party. I also represented the United States at the opening of Parliament. I read a proclamation from the President of the United States at a big ceremony held in the biggest cathedral in Bermuda each Thanksgiving and every Veteran's DayI laid a wreath at the grave of an American who died in the War of 1812.

Whenever I gave a dinner party I would ask one of the guests of honor to propose a toast to the President of the United States. Then I would stand and toast ``the Queen''. Ned Johnson, the chairman of Fidelity, and a big Republican, was guest of honor at a dinner party I held for 24 people. I asked him to lead the toast to the President of the United States. This dinner took place right after the mid-term elections in 1994 when Democrats had suffered a big defeat and Republicans took over control of the U.S. House for the first time in decades. He tapped his glass to get everyone's attention and they said: `` A toast, to the President ... and Congress of the United States.''

It is not easy to break into society in Bermuda. There are a lot of very wealthy Americans who live on the island who never get invited to the ``A'' list parties of Bermudians.

LIVING IN PARADISE ➤

Because of my position, I was invited to a lot of dinners. As Consul General, I was always seated next to the hostess and I made many good friends.

I invited Hugh Barit, a financier, and his wife, Gigi, to dinner one night at Chelston. Hugh and his wife had had a disagreement so Gigi stayed home. During dinner, a piece of roast beef got caught in my throat and I began to choke. As I gasped for air and turned blue, Hugh grabbed me in the Heimlich maneuver and the piece of meat popped free allowing me to breathe again. I fortunately was fine but they took me to the hospital just to make sure.

The next day, I sent two dozen red roses to his house as a thank you with a note saying: ``Thanks for the best hug I ever had." His wife accepted the delivery and evidently thought the flowers were for her, a makeup gesture from Hugh. I'm not sure what she thought was going on when she read that note to her husband signed by ``Bob", the gay U.S. Consul General.

One of the highlights of my time in Bermuda came towards the end, my 60th birthday party in September of 1998. Patricia Barry Pettit, a close friend, did the planning. Patricia is the widow of Tom Pettit, the NBC newsman who died in 1995 not long after retiring to Bermuda. We became very dear friends and she generously acted as a hostess at many of my dinner parties. I was very touched that 220 friends and relatives came from off island to attend along with 150 Bermudians. Everyone arrived on Friday night and we went on a sunset cruise around the island with an

THE MONEY GUY

open bar. We had dinner at a hotel nightclub. Jimmy Keys, Bermuda's best known musician and entertainer, sang. We held a golf tournament the next day and on Saturday night hosted a huge black tie dinner at Chelston beneath an enormous tent down by the water. A train took people up and down the hill from the main house to the tent and violinists played from the balcony as the guests arrived at the house. The Bermuda marching band opened the speaking program at the tent.

The party was spectacular.

I received very special birthday wishes on a DVD that opened with an image of the Presidential Seal. First Vice President Al Gore, then First Lady Hillary Rodham Clinton and then President Bill Clinton addressed me and my guests via video.

Each greeting was more gracious than the other but I was particularly touched by President Clinton's remarks because his words were so personal.

``I remember flying up from Arkansas to your 50th birthday celebration in Boston,'' he said. ``Many presidential candidates showed up for that party hoping to make an impression and win your help some day. Three years later when I was still trying to decide to run, I heard you were in Little Rock. I wasn't sure what it meant but it sure made headlines in the Washington Post. After you arrived, things began to move fast. Then I experienced what everyone in politics knows, Bob Farmer gets results. I will always remember those who were on board when only Hillary and my mother thought I had a chance." I learned afterwards that the President taped that message on a particularly stressful day at the White House. That September was when Kenneth Starr's Report with all its salacious details on the president's relationship with Monica Lewinsky was released by Congress and went up on the Internet. The President reportedly insisted upon doing the video because it was for me.

A typical posting for an ambassadorial appointee is three years and I fully expected to go back to the United States after three years. My friends in Bermuda began to host a series of good-bye parties. At a particularly lovely lunch at a yacht club, I was told the White House had called and I needed to return the call immediately. I got to the phone and checked in. I was asked if I would be willing to stay on a little longer. Naturally, I said yes. I then went back to the luncheon and told them they were not getting rid of me yet. So my tenure was extended for another 18 months. There was a lot of joking among my friends about my long goodbye.

But after my birthday party in the fall of 1998, I was really ready to go home. I had a touch of island fever. The lifestyle was amazing but there is something very limited about living on an island for an extended period of time. There is only so much you can do and so many people you can do it with. I was restless. The U.S. government put Chelston up for sale and my visitors began to dwindle. My closest friends and relatives visited for the birthday party in September and it was hard for them to justify another trip right away.

I had bought a new condominium in Miami in a pre-construction phase and was arranging for its furnishing long distance and anxious to get back to Florida fulltime. So in March of 1999, I went home.

I felt very grateful to have the opportunity to represent the United States in Bermuda. Bermuda treated me very well. David White OBE, the editor of the Royal Gazette, a very distinguished gentleman who became a great friend, kindly I had ``done a magnificent job for his country.''

`` No previous Consul General and certainly no Bermudian public figure in recent times had managed to make so many friends and such a wide range of contacts throughout Bermuda,'' said the editorial which quoted the leaders of both political parties saying they would miss me. ``Bob Farmer,'' said the editorial, ``is the quintessential hard act to follow.''

On that note, I was glad to ``retire'' from public service and headed back to Miami for the next phase of my life.

CHAPTER 8

The Final Campaigns

I returned to Miami and, for the first time in 20 years, sat out a presidential campaign. While still in Bermuda, I was asked to visit Vice President Al Gore and flew up to Washington to meet with him at the vice president's official residence on Massachusetts Avenue. But his fundraising team was already in place leaving no role for me. In any case, after five years of public service, it was time for me to make some money and spend time getting my life back in order. I became involved in some business ventures including an internet start-up.

Upon my return I also became involved in the first long term relationship since I broke up with Tim McNeill. I met Tommy Winston while he was working as a physical therapist in Florida. Tommy is a tremendous athlete with a beautiful Irish tenor voice. He was a kick boxing champion in his native Ireland when he was younger. When I met him, he had been in a relationship with a 78-year-old man for eight years. His companion had a heart attack and died

THE MONEY GUY

while he and Tommy were my house guests. Tommy went back to Ireland for some time and when he returned, we started living together. Tommy is an exceptionally kind and gentle person who is very popular with my friends despite the 30 year age difference. He is often asked to sing at parties. Because he does not drink, we joke that we get a lot of social invitations because he can act as designated driver. It is a great comfort to have such a wonderful companion by my side as I grow older.

Not too long after the 2000 recount debacle when the Supreme Court effectively stole the election for George W. Bush, the jockeying began for 2004. It was clear that Massachusetts Senator John F. Kerry intended to run. John and I had been friends since his election as lieutenant governor in Massachusetts in 1982, the year of the famous re-match campaign between Mike Dukakis and Ed King. I called Clay Constantinou in 2001 and told him Kerry was the man for 2004. Clay thought I was nuts because no one thought another Northeast liberal, particularly one from Massachusetts, had a prayer of a chance.

John invited me to lunch at the historic Senate Dining Room in the U.S. Capitol, one of the most exclusive dining rooms in Washington, and I asked him if I could bring along Clay. The Senate Dining Room is where Senators bring their guests so you cannot look around without seeing a newsmaker. As we were leaving, we ran into Hillary Clinton who was then the Senator from New York. She said, ``This must be an important meeting if the two of you are here.''

THE FINAL CAMPAIGNS

Later that day, we had dinner with John and Teresa at their home on O Street in Georgetown. When Clay left the room, I told John, ``I know it is illegal to ask for a job, but I want you to know that I am still interested in public service and particularly interested in being Ambassador to the Court of St. James.'' I had always wanted to be the U.S. Ambassador to England, even during the Dukakis campaign. It is the ultimate prize for a political fundraiser. When I first expressed that ambition years before, Tim McNeill quipped, ``That's just what England needs, another Queen who can't dress.''

Sometime after the 2004 election, I called John Kerry and said, ``John, I worked very hard for you on the campaign and spent two years of my life dedicated to the cause so I think I have the right to ask you what position I might have been given had you been successful.''

John replied, ``I remember the conversation we had in my library when you first signed on expressing an interest in Ambassador to the Court of St. James. I don't know if you would have gotten that because you have a special set of skills and I may have wanted you in Washington but I can assure you that you would have been very happy with the job you received.''

I was very pleased by that response so I called my friend John Sasso and repeated the conversation to him. John Sasso burst out laughing. I said, ``Why are you laughing?'' And he said, ``Because obviously, he has not spent a second thinking about it!'' So I called back John Kerry and told

◄ **THE MONEY GUY**

him what Sasso said. John acted insulted and huffed,``Of course, I thought about it'' and promptly switched the subject. We never spoke about that again. I again called Sasso, and when he burst out laughing this time, it dawned on me that Sasso, who always had great respect for Kerry, had been kidding me and playing to my ego when he said Kerry probably hadn't thought much about a position for me.

John Forbes Kerry was one of those golden boys who seemed destined for greatness. He was a graduate of Yale, the descendent of one of the oldest families in Massachusetts and a combat war hero with a Silver and Bronze Star for valor who became a leader a leader of Vietnam Veterans against the War. John, like his hero John F. Kennedy, was bright, articulate and talented, and many assumed that someday he would be in the White House just like the other JFK. He testified against the war in Viet Nam before the Senate Foreign Relations Committee in 1971 in a dazzling performance that made him an overnight political sensation. He wore military fatigues to the hearing and memorably asked, ``How do you ask a man to be the last man to die for a mistake?'' His career path took a lot of twists and turns before he finally had his shot at the presidency in 2004 and I was happy to be part of it.

By the time I met John, he and his first wife Julia had separated and he was romantically involved with his former law partner, Roanne Sragow, a gorgeous blonde who

THE FINAL CAMPAIGNS

was as kind and intelligent as she was beautiful. John and Roanne and Tim McNeill and I dined regularly at the old Ritz-Carlton Hotel, one of the city's most elegant hotels across from the Boston Public Garden on Arlington Street. When I won at gin rummy, I invited them to be my guests so we had dinner together nearly every week. We always ordered profiteroles for dessert because John loved them. He is one of those long lean people who never gain an ounce regardless of what he eats.

Some years later, Governor Dukakis appointed Roanne to the District Court bench. She and John had gone their separate ways. Ro always wanted to have a family and she has been happily married for many years to Richard Licht, the former lieutenant governor of Rhode Island. They have two beautiful children. She is still one of my favorite people and a dear friend.

One day, Roanne was presiding in court and a guilty defendant, furious over the prison sentence she just imposed, whirled around as he left the courtroom and shouted, ``Fuck you, Judge!'' Without missing a beat, Roanne smartly slammed down her gavel and snapped: ``Motion denied!'' I always thought that story captured Roanne and her quick wit.

So we spent a lot of time together. Tim and I went sailing with John and Roanne in the Caribbean just before John took the oath of office as a U.S. Senator in 1985. I asked him, ``John, if I am ever nominated for a high position in government, will you vote to confirm me?'' He said, ``Of

THE MONEY GUY

course not. I'm much too patriotic." I have a photograph of me snapped by Tim in which I am pretending to strangle him after that remark.

And John crashed more than once at my condo in Washington. Despite his pedigree, his branch of the Forbes family had run out of money years before and John was between apartments. My hospitality got him in some political trouble when Governor William Weld challenged him for the Senate seat in 1996 and made an issue of John staying at my condo while I was working for a lobbying firm. Anyone who knows me knows the hospitality was innocent and extended out of friendship. John was welcome to stay with me whenever he wanted just as any friend was. It had nothing to do with my work at Cassidy where I was a rainmaker. In fact, because of our long standing relationship, I could tease him in a way no one else dared. I have fond memories of playing gin rummy with him on his campaign plane and jokingly insulting him much to the horror of his aides.

Fundraisers tend to be competitive people. In fact, the only thing two fundraisers can ever agree on is how much a third fundraiser should give. In my experience, the best fundraisers are extremely successful in their professional lives. They are well-to-do businessmen and lawyers with healthy egos, lots of ambition and drive, and generally quite smart. I tried to nurture a positive atmosphere and spread around credit and praise to make everyone feel included and valued. And while a new fundraiser may be

THE FINAL CAMPAIGNS

content to be a lieutenant in a first campaign, without exception, they always want to be captains and generals in the next campaign. We used that competitive spirit in the Kerry campaign in Massachusetts by posting a Leader Board to track the amount each fundraiser raised by the week. We posted the results every Monday. On Sunday night, some of the best fundraisers in the state would call in with last minute checks to report to boost their position on the board the following morning. Jon Patsavos, the finance director for John in Massachusetts, did an exceptional job in helping raise the seed money for the campaign.

But some people could always be counted on to bring out the knives. I learned much later that an innocent social dinner was used against me during the Clinton campaign.

I had become very fond of Dick Gephardt and his wife Jane. Dick was the House Majority Leader and we enjoyed one another's company. During Bill Clinton's 1992 campaign for the presidency, the campaign was nearly undone by the allegations of 12 year sexual affair made by Gennifer Flowers, a worse for wear cabaret singer from Arkansas. Clinton overcame the controversy and went on to win the Democratic nomination, but during that rocky time, I happened to be in Washington and invited Dick and Jane to join me for dinner at The Palm Restaurant in Washington. Now, if I was up to anything sneaky, the last place I would schedule a rendezvous would be The Palm, a power-dining spot on 19th Street in downtown Washington where everyone goes to see and be seen. I later learned that the innocent social dinner was used by my rivals to spread the rumor I was trying to convince Dick to get into the Democratic Presidential race to take advantage of the vulnerable Clinton. Nothing could be further from the truth. But to this day there are people who still maintain I betrayed Bill Clinton at that critical time in the race. Fortunately, Clinton never gave the rumor any credence.

For the 2004 race Kerry named me national treasurer of his presidential campaign and it was my job to recruit members of the national finance committee and to make them feel good and part of the campaign. John had plenty of supporters and relationships dating back to his time in the U.S. Navy and his more recent stint as chairman of the Democratic Senatorial Campaign Committee which raised money to help elect Democratic members of the U.S. Senate. But every presidential candidate has extreme demands upon his time. I stepped in as a surrogate to create a fundraising family for John Kerry. I held more than 2,500 one-on-one meetings all over the country over a two year period often doing as many as 8 to 10 meetings a day.

I often told potential finance committee members the story of Milton A. Wolf. He was a successful developer of shopping centers and homes in Cleveland Ohio. He became involved in Jimmy Carters' 1976 campaign very early. .

I told people about Milton. ``Milton was a home builder but he raised $25,000 for Jimmy Carter early on. You pick

THE FINAL CAMPAIGNS

up the Wall Street Journal one day and see Milton got a major presidential appointment. You might say, ` why him and not me? I'm more successful than he is. I'm smarter than he is.' It's very simple. He became a player. He got involved and he helped Carter early. Presidents never forget the guys who get involved early on. It is not a given that many people have the ability to raise serious money. But you do have that ability. If you don't use it you are wasting your talent by not getting involved." A grateful President remembered Milton's key support at a time he needed it most and named him Ambassador Extraordinary and Plenipotentiary of the United States to Austria.

Everyone wants to feel important and reminding these successful people that they could be even more successful was like dangling catnip before a feral cat. It has been my experience that successful people are always looking for another mountain to climb. I told potential committee members how accessible politics is at the very highest levels. I told them how to get involved and how their involvement would be recognized if the candidate was successful. I also told them that making a commitment early before the candidacy takes off is really important.

I would tell them, `` John Kerry doesn't have a lot of friends" in Florida or Arizona or Illinois or wherever I happened to be. ``You can become a major player for him in this state. At the end of the day, when people are recognizing supporters a lot of it has to do with geography. You won't find ten appointees or White House guests from the

THE MONEY GUY

same state. The new administration spreads around the gratitude and thanks. Since he doesn't have made friends in your state, you can become a leader in your state.''

I always encouraged them to develop a good relationship with their home state Senators, too, because a President-elect needs Senators to get his legislation and appointees through Congress. For contributors with an interest in public service, I reminded them that Senators can wield a lot of influence over appointments as well. I explained the process of rewards and recognition and acted as a rabbi to the prominent fundraisers.

One night after an event at John's home in Boston, I got a call telling me that John Kerry had a breakfast meeting the following morning with a major private equity investor who had promised he would raise $5 million in return for being named national finance chairman. I was aghast. I called John and finally reached him at 11 p.m. that night and told him there was no way anyone could raise that much money. I advised him to say. ``I'm sure you will be a great asset to my team. Why don't you begin by raising $250,000 and we will talk about a more significant role for you in the campaign.'' He did just that and the guy raised about $10,000.

Even the best in the business cannot raise $5 million by themselves. To me, if someone promises something that is not achievable, he is totally full of hot air. I knew the equity investor had never raised money for a campaign. In my experience, if someone promises the moon, he probably does not understand the process. If the bar is set too high, fundraisers will get discouraged after five phone calls and give up. It is much better to ask people to raise $5,000. If they raise $10,000 put them on the state finance committee. If they raise $25,000, name them to the national finance committee. Each goal is realistic and achievable. During my travels around the country for John Kerry, I would start every meeting by asking the potential donor to tell me about himself. We did not do Google searches on people back then so I would say, ``I've heard about you but I do not know you well. Tell me a little bit about yourself. Where did you go to school? How many kids do you have? Tell me how you became so successful in business?'' I would ask for a two or three minute bio but my experience is most people love talking about themselves and they would go on for some time. It was a great way to break the ice and show my interest in them.

During those meetings, I would hand my Blackberry and cell phone to my able assistant, Justin Erlich. Justin had his own Blackberry and cell phone and he would line up four devices on the table in front of him. If my phone rang, he answered it. If it was an important call, regardless of who was calling, he was supposed to say ``Excuse me but John Kerry is on the line and needs to speak to you.'' No one could be offended by an interruption if the candidate himself needed my attention. That was my cue to leave the table and take the call.

During one meeting, my personal cell phone rang and

THE MONEY GUY

Justin answered it. He told me it was John Kerry. I excused myself to take the call. As we walked away from the table, I asked Justin who was on the phone. He said, ``John Kerry.'' I said, ``No, who is on the phone.'' He said, ``It really is John Kerry!'' We went on like Alphonse and Gaston until I realized it was, in fact, John Kerry on the phone.

I have never been too conscientious about my health despite the best efforts of my friends and colleagues. Both of my parents smoked and lived into their 80's and 90's so I am blessed with excellent genes. Justin remembers he kept me supplied with a steady supply of Pepsi Cola at my insistence. I refused to drink the diet Pepsi. My friends worried about the pace of my travel and from time to time would gang up on me and insist I take a spa break to get away from the cigarettes and rich food of the road. Justin and I went down to Florida for just such a spa break during the Kerry campaign. Every morning, I insisted he pick me up at the luxurious spa and drive me to my Miami condo to make phone calls and then have him drive me back later in the day. Needless to say, those periodic breaks did not make a bit of difference.

There was a no smoking rule at the Kerry campaign headquarters in Washington so I would go down to the sidewalk to smoke a cigarette. John Kerry went by in a car one day and saw me smoking out front. He called and left a message on my cell phone. ``Bob,'' he said in a mock stern tone,`` I just saw you smoking down front. You promised to give up smoking and this apparently is a flip flop. All this campaign needs is another flip flopper. This could destroy my campaign. " And he hung up. It was another demonstration of his wry sense of humor.

The Kerry campaign signaled a momentous change for fundraisers like me. Howard Dean, the Governor of Vermont, became an overnight political sensation because of the stunning amount of money he raised via the Internet. During an early Kerry campaign meeting at Teresa Heinz Kerry's seaside home on Nantucket, the political operatives thought Howard Dean's success on raising money through the Internet was a onetime thing that would never be repeated. I disagreed. I had built my first business successes in direct mail and marketing and I thought they were mistaken and said so at the time. In campaign fundraising, ``the list' of contributors is everything. Once someone gives, they are more likely to give again. Having a computerized list of givers was a huge plus for Dean.

Kerry's first campaign manager was Jim Jordan, a very smart and articulate political operative. At our first national finance committee meeting, I asked him to speak and he walked into a room of men wearing business suits and ties in an open collar shirt, blue jeans and cowboy boots, his signature look. As is often the case, the first campaign manager gets blamed for all the early problems in a campaign and does not survive. Jim was replaced by Mary Beth Cahill, a former chief of staff to Senator Kennedy who recommended her to John. We had a cordial relationship until Kurt Wagar, our vice chairman from Florida gave a press interview which she did not like. She wanted to fire him. I defended him and said, ``Look, all of our finance chairs are well connected to the press and you can't stop them from talking to reporters. Most of them are pretty sophisticated.'' Kurt was a prominent Florida attorney. She got angry with me. And said, ``I can't talk about this anymore'' and slammed down the phone. That was the last conversation I had with her during the campaign. She was never willing to meet with major fundraisers. Milton Ferrell, our Florida state finance chair, wanted to meet with her and she said she was too busy. Another time one of her assistants sent an email to the entire campaign staff informing us that if we saw Mary Beth outside the office we were not to speak to her because she was too busy and had other things on her mind. During a question and answer session with students at the Kennedy School at Harvard the following year, John Edwards was asked the one lesson he learned in 2004. He said, ``Don't listen to Mary Beth Cahill.'' That was quite a statement for him to make, particularly given Cahill was present at the time.

But long before that as 2003 wound down, John Kerry's campaign seemed stuck in first gear. Bob Crowe, one of John's best friends and a senior member of the finance committee, remembers vividly how we were all making non-stop phone calls to everyone we knew around the country during those final months of 2003 and getting very, very few responses. In fact, many times we could not get people on the phone to take our calls.

THE FINAL CAMPAIGNS ➤

In December of 2003, John made a decision to use his house in Louisburg Square in Boston as collateral for a $6.4 million loan for the campaign. He had married Teresa Heinz, the widow of Senator John Heinz who was the heir to the Heinz catsup fortune in 1995, so he technically had access to a lot of her family money. But he did not want to use his wife's money. When they married in 1995, they bought a former convent in Louisburg Square, a private square in the heart of the exclusive and historic Beacon Hill neighborhood in Boston. Teresa had the building gutted and completely rebuilt into a comfortable and elegant town home that looked as though it had been there for 100 years. Their kitchen soared several stories high where the convent chapel had once been located. John had an office at the very top of the house with a spiral staircase to the roof where he would often sit and look at the city lights of Boston. Using the house to borrow money showed his commitment to the campaign and signaled the problems we were having keeping up with the Internet powerhouse unleashed by Dean. I advised him not to do it because the house was his most valuable asset and at the end of the day his children's inheritance. But he went ahead. He made the right call because it kept the campaign afloat for the final weeks before the Iowa caucuses.

In the third quarter finance reports, we killed ourselves to raise just under $4 million. Dean raised $14.8 million. We were flying all over the country begging people one at a time for money while a computer geek at the Dean campaign clicked a mouse and set off a tsunami of millions of

◄ THE MONEY GUY

dollars in contributions that averaged less than $80 each. Not only was raising money on the Internet cost effective because there was virtually no overhead, but each person who gave $80 could give another $80 and another $80 until reaching the maximum donation of $2,000. Internet givers were unquestionably the gift that kept on giving.

Fortunately, John proved to be the better candidate than Dean. About two weeks before the Iowa caucuses, the entire finance committee flew to Iowa to go door to door and do whatever we could to help John. Our phone calls were not getting returned so we decided we would go into the field and do whatever we could for our candidate. We had a wonderful time. It was a unique experience for most members of the committee. Bob Crowe says Kerry told him to leave his elegant English tailored shirts at home and wear his L.L. Bean gear. We were booked into a hotel in Cedar Rapids called the Five Seasons. Bob Crowe remembers his secretary telling him he was staying at a Four Seasons Hotel. Bob actually lives in a luxury condominium built above the Four Seasons Hotel in Boston so he is familiar with the Four Seasons brand and he was a little skeptical, particularly given the room rate was $99 a night. The ``Five Seasons'' was run by a more budget friendly hotel chain.

We all went out to dinner one night to one of the ``best'' restaurant in town, a place called the Steak & Chop. We had a grand time and ordered many drinks and bottles of wine, told stories and recounted our adventures knocking on doors in Cedar Rapids where the nicest people in the

THE FINAL CAMPAIGNS

world invited us in for chocolate chip cookies and coffee. Lou Susman, the campaign finance chair, had offered to pick up the tab but he left early so I ended up splitting the bill with Bob Crowe. It was an expensive dinner.

You cannot imagine how it felt as the returns began to roll into Des Moines the night of the Iowa caucuses. We were elated and a bit inebriated when John won the Iowa caucuses in a decisive upset. He pulled down 37.6 percent of the vote followed by John Edwards at 31.8 percent, Howard Dean at 18 percent and Dick Gephardt at 10.6.

Governor Dean shrieked during his speech that night in an effort to rally his supporters. Unfortunately for him, the Dean Scream as it came known made him look unhinged on national television. The Scream went viral on both cable TV and the Internet and his third place showing in Iowa effectively ended his campaign that night though he struggled on for another month before withdrawing in February after a dismal showing in Wisconsin.

The day after the Iowa caucus, our fundraising phone calls were returned. Bob Crowe remembers he received 122 telephone calls on January 20, 2004, the day after the Iowa caucuses, and every single caller said, ``Gee, I've been meaning to call you back but I've been so busy with the holiday season. The check is in the mail.'' Nothing works like success in politics.

Within days, we raised enough money to pay off the mortgage John took out on the Louisburg Square house.

◄ THE MONEY GUY

Unless you have lived through a campaign, you cannot appreciate the tensions and the extraordinary emotional ups and downs of a presidential campaign. It is as if a 25 year corporate history was compressed in one year with every hiring, firing, victory and loss taking place in a matter of months. One crisis for me came when John called me one day and told me he had recruited Lou Susman, a Chicago businessman. I said, ``Great.'' He said, ``He is going to be finance chairman of the campaign.'' He had never discussed it with me in advance. Obviously, the candidate had the right to name whom he wanted but Susman and I had very different styles. Lou could be very charming but also he was as tough as nails. Lou grew up St. Louis, Missouri where he was a lawyer in a prestigious St. Louis law firm and a director of the St. Louis Cardinals. He moved to Chicago in 1989 and became vice chairman of Citigroup Corporation and Investment Banking. Lou had raised money for Democrats for years and had a no holds barred aggressive demeanor. He was nicknamed ``The Vacuum Cleaner'' for his ability to hoover up money but he also could have been called ``The Bull Dozer'' for the way he crushed anyone who stood in his way.

Lou and I shared the same ambition: to be Ambassador to the Court of St. James, one of the most desirable postings if Kerry won the White House so that probably contributed to the tension between us. Lou eventually secured that job from President Obama. Lou was very close to Penny Pritzker who was Obama's finance chair. My friends in London tell me Lou is one of the best ambassadors in

THE FINAL CAMPAIGNS

memory and has done commendable work representing our country in England.

Every campaign attracts ambitious people who hope to ride the campaign straight to a high ranking government position and the Kerry campaign had its share. My experience is when people close their doors in a campaign, it probably means they are plotting about which job they want to get if and when the candidate wins.

One evening, I invited a number of fundraisers to dinner in Washington with Arianna Huffington, the co-founder of The Huffington Post who endorsed John in 2004. John Martilla, a longtime Boston based political consultant and an old friend of John's dating back to John's first unsuccessful campaign for Congress in 1972, was with us. In the course of the dinner, someone raised the issue of whether John would opt out of the federal matching money system. By deciding to forego federal matching money, a candidate could spend as much as he could raise. By accepting the federal match, the candidate agreed to a spending ceiling in each state. John eventually opted out of the system in 2004 for the primary season because it would have been political suicide to accept limits given Howard Deans' decision to spend as much as he needed to win but at that point no decision had been made. The issue came up over dinner as a matter of idle speculation and was part of ongoing gossip over the campaign.

I received a phone call later that night from Cam Kerry, John's younger brother who was quite concerned about

◄ **THE MONEY GUY**

the dinner based upon a report from Martilla. Martilla had attended a high level staff meeting after our dinner and told Cam we had discussed the issue in front of Arianna Huffington.

I was so upset that I stayed up most of the night drafting a letter of resignation. I was just about to send it to John Kerry the next morning when John called and told me not to worry. We talked about six more times and I agreed to stay on board though I did insist on reading the letter of resignation to him because I put a lot of effort and emotion into what I felt was an eloquent letter. The issue blew over. Arianna, by the way, never went public with our dinner conversation. I learned an important lesson that night about trust. Cam and I remained good friends. He has always been a source of steady advice to his big brother and is now serving as general counsel at the U.S. Department of Commerce. And, in fact, John Martilla and I also bonded over similar medical issues years later and became good friends.

The 2004 campaign was the first one in which I actively courted the gay community for contributions as an openly gay man. At one fundraiser in Fort Lauderdale for the Kerry campaign, Teresa Heinz Kerry delivered a very compassionate speech in which she talked about being a mother and how every child deserved to be loved equally regardless of sexual orientation. Congressman Barney Frank was standing next to me. At the conclusion of the speech, she spoke about meeting a young gay man at another event who said,`` I wish you had been my mother."

THE FINAL CAMPAIGNS

Barney said, looked at me and said, ``Who wouldn't want her for a mother? She's worth a billion dollars.'' Barney overstated Teresa's net worth but the point was well taken.

Teresa Heinz Kerry is a fascinating combination of exotic beauty and fierce intelligence. She grew up in Mozambique where her father, a native of Portugal, was a medical doctor. She lost her first husband, Senator John Heinz, the sole heir to the Heinz food fortune, just weeks before their 25th wedding anniversary when his private plane collided with a helicopter. She and John Kerry met years later through their shared passion for the environment. Teresa has no interest in being the dutiful and conventional political wife. She has made a mark as a philanthropist by demanding those who receive bequests of her money produce results, a policy that effectively changed the style of philanthropy in the United States.

John wrapped up the Democratic nomination very quickly in 2004. It meant he would have months to prepare for the general election campaign against George W. Bush in November. But first he needed to select a running mate. Peter Maroney, the Kerry finance director, and I pushed for Dick Gephardt. I had always admired him and thought he would be a terrific candidate. One day Peter and I were scheduled to speak to 250 trial lawyers who all wanted John Edwards to be on the ticket. Just before we spoke, I turned to Peter and said, ``Remember where the car is, we may be running for it.'' Peter is a good looking outgoing Philadelphia native who had devoted ten years of his life

THE MONEY GUY

as finance director for John Kerry's campaigns. We often knocked heads on that campaign but ended up as good friends.

Some key members of the fundraising team wanted Edwards to be the Vice Presidential candidate. Edwards, the U.S. Senator from North Carolina, had been a very successful trial lawyer before his election. He was a handsome and charismatic politician with a compelling personal story. His chief fundraiser was a wonderful Texas lawyer named Fred Baron. Fred was a legal legend. He brought the first asbestos law suit and essentially created the class action lawsuit industry in America. He also made a fortune. Fred was a powerfully effective fundraiser. He knew every trial lawyer in the country and used his skill to raise money for his candidate. When Edwards got out of the race, we decided that Rodney Margol, the co-vice chair of our finance committee and a talented trial lawyer from Florida, should make the approach. I met Rodney at a fundraiser in Fort Lauderdale. Rodney had been a Kerry fan since 1971. As an undergraduate, he invited Kerry to speak at his college. They spent the weekend hanging out together and Rodney had followed his career ever since.

When I first met Rodney, he told me that he had known John for more than 30 years and felt he might be able to put together $10,000 for his campaign. He remembers I smiled at him and said, ``You can do $25,000.'' He was good. After the Iowa caucus, I persuaded Rodney to move to Washington to work fulltime on fundraising. The first night he was in town, I invited him to join me at The Palm for dinner. He agreed and then I mentioned we would be joined by ``two lady friends.'' Rodney was privately dismayed because he was afraid his wife would find out and be furious. He had left her back in Florida where their youngest son was still in high school and his first night in town he would be going out with me and ``two lady friends.'' He was relieved to discover the ``two lady friends'' were former Secretary of State Madeleine Albright and former Chief of Protocol Molly Raiser.

That reminds me of one of my favorite fundraising stories. When Terry McAuliffe served as chairman of the Democratic National Committee, he went to see Bren Simon, who was married to one of the owners of the Simon Property Group, the largest public real estate company in the United States. He asked her to contribute $1 million to the Party and she readily agreed handing him a check for $1 million. As he left her house, he paused at the door and looked at his aide and asked, ``Did I leave something on the table?''

Rodney called Fred Baron several times but Fred was not ready to talk until Edwards finally officially withdrew from contention after Super Tuesday. Fred told him he needed two weeks of mourning and flew to Paris with his wife and law partner Lisa Blue-Baron. He called when he returned and joined us, sharing an office in Washington with Rodney. Fred was a powerful champion for Edwards to be the vice presidential nominee and many of the finance committee members were persuaded.

◄ **THE MONEY GUY**

Fred Baron tragically died much too young of cancer at the age of 61 in 2008. I must note that in 2004, Edwards was still happily married to Elizabeth Edwards. His affair with Rielle Hunter and the out of wedlock baby he fathered were years in the future. But looking back, I have to say none of us could have predicted Edwards would be so indiscreet or self-destructive. Anyone who decides to run for President needs to meet a high standard for behavior and clearly Edwards came up short. I have always been surprised at the personal shortcomings of public figures. Nobody asks anyone to run for public office and if you make that decision, you should understand your behavior is going to be scrutinized closely. Anyone can call the press on you. Gary Hart's presidential campaign collapsed when he was photographed with an attractive woman who was not his wife sitting in his lap on the boat the Monkey Business.

When I first moved to Washington as treasurer of DNC, a friend invited me to a gay bar. A week later, a reporter for the Boston Globe said he heard I had been at the bar. I hadn't seen anyone I knew that night, but realized that as treasurer of the DNC, I should not be seen in gay bars. So I never went to another gay bar while I was in Washington.

The 2004 general election proved to be difficult. The Republicans attacked John's war record which still makes me shake my head. George W. Bush enlisted in the Texas National Guard to avoid the draft during the Vietnam War and then did not even show up for all of his training. John Kerry enlisted in the U.S. Navy, served as a naval officer, distinguished himself in combat, was wounded and earned two of the highest military honors. Yet the Republicans managed to smear him and use his service against him. After the way Bush's father's campaign maligned Michael Dukakis in 1988 for his commitment to civil liberties as a ``card carrying member of the ACLU'' and for the exploits of a Massachusetts prison inmate Willie Horton who had escaped while on a furlough program and assaulted a woman in Maryland. I would have thought it impossible for it to happen again but it did. The Swift Boat ads showed the power of advertising and the ability of ads to distort the facts and how free media stories on the ad can exaggerate the influence of a small advertising buy. The ad buy was only $250,000 and it was in August. Kerry's advisers told him not to respond and hang onto his money for later in the campaign because the public doesn't like negative ads.

In hindsight, that was a big mistake because he was still being defined to the American public in August. Most voters knew very little about him. He should have gone public in an aggressive way and challenged George W. Bush to compare military records if that was what he wanted to do.

After John won the nomination, I sat down with Terry McAuliffe, then the chairman of the Democratic National Committee and a formidable fundraiser in his own right. He wanted us to call together five of the top fundraisers and run a boiler plate operation and call as many people as possible to raise money for the DNC for the general

◄ **THE MONEY GUY**

election. Terry is one of the most entertaining and charming people in the world. He later ran for public office himself in Virginia. He was not successful but he was always a great colleague. I suggested that instead we create a trustee program where each trustee would promise to try to raise $250,000 in $25,000 donations. I hoped to get 200 trustees. Within a month, we signed up 600 who committed to raise the quarter million dollars. Half of them actually achieved this feat. A couple of New Yorkers actually raised $1 million each for the party.

We held a big party for the trustees at Teresa Heinz Kerry's wonderful farm outside of Pittsburgh. We set up a big tent on the grounds and as master of ceremonies I acknowledged the contribution of virtually every single person there as John stood behind me. The group included more than 40 state finance chairs. I was a little concerned that I went on too long. He told me afterwards that he liked it because he waved and recognized each person as I named him. And the fundraisers were delighted to see their hard work recognized by the candidate. Walter Shorenstein who was then 89 attended and I made an effort to recognize a very special person who came all the way from California to be with us.

We then launched a program for people under the age of 40 with a goal of raising $100,000. The program was a big success and got a lot of younger people involved in the party.

We had some difficult times during that campaign. During

THE FINAL CAMPAIGNS

the dog days of August when the Swift Boat attacks were relentless and tempers were flaring, Peter Maroney and I got into a few battles. Finally, John Sasso brought us into a room at the Democratic National Committee and drew up a formal treaty for us to sign. It said we were to respect one another's views, opinions and ideas. We would treat one another with respect and civility and we would work together for the common goal. He made us sign it and he taped it up on his wall. I have to say it worked!

By Election Day, we were feeling positive about John's prospects. We all flew back to Boston on the Gulfstream of Milton Ferrell, our Florida finance chair, for a reception at the Copley Plaza Hotel in the Back Bay. Milton was a man of great personal integrity and courage. Milton Ferrell was such a stand up guy that he went to bat for a young finance committee staff member when a senior person wanted to throw the young man under the bus for something that was not his fault. Although the incident took place late in the campaign when most people are leery of rocking the boat, Milt called John Kerry directly to defend the young staff member and saved his job. As we got off the plane, we all clicked on our Blackberries to get the reports of network exit polls being conducted throughout the nation. The early exit polls showed John winning the election so by the time we gathered for the reception at 4:30 p.m., we were beginning to celebrate. The media pool resources to conduct exit polls which are taken of people as they leave the polls. They traditionally had been extremely accurate. Bob Shrum, the Democratic

199

THE MONEY GUY

political consultant, turned to John and said, ``Let me be the first to call you Mr. President.'' We were giddy until television commentators started to warn things were not as they seemed about 7:30 p.m. Then everything went downhill. We soared to the heights of joy and plunged just as quickly to the depths of disappointment. Bush only won by two percentage points and my home state of Ohio proved to be pivotal.

This loss was particularly crushing because I strongly felt George W. Bush was bad for the country and John Kerry would have made a superior President. The next morning, we had arranged for a breakfast for the finance committee and virtually no one showed up. Once the campaign is over, it is over.

The 2008 campaign opened up the opportunity for a Democratic victory because Bush would not be running for reelection, the economy was tanking and the wars in Iraq and Afghanistan were growing more unpopular by the day. Many of the key Kerry fundraisers were in a difficult position because he flirted seriously with running again and asked me and others not to commit to anyone until he made a decision. I respected that but my experience has been that you must be involved in a campaign from the very beginning. The candidate and his key advisors always remember those who were with them at the kickoff and latecomers are tolerated but not loved.

The Democratic Party differs from the Republican Party in one important way; the Democrats don't believe in second

THE FINAL CAMPAIGNS

chances. On the Republican side, Richard Nixon, George H. W. Bush and Ronald Reagan won the presidency on a second try. But once a Democratic nominee loses, that is it. John finally announced in January of 2007 that he would not get into the race. At that early juncture, Senators Hillary Rodham Clinton and Barack Obama were the heavyweights in the field but the insider money was with Hillary.

Hillary did not reach out to me or others on the Kerry team. That surprised us. We had demonstrated a very successful fundraising operation in 2004. But as I reflect back her failure to contact us probably wasn't too surprising. She had put together a great fundraising team for her Senate race and New York, along with California, is one of the best sources of dollars for Democratic candidates. One thing that I have noticed is that once a team has been established, the team has a vested interest in maintaining their own position. As a result, the leaders of the fundraising team are not always receptive to bringing on new high profile fundraisers even to the detriment of the campaign. Hillary's campaign team was particularly tight knit and not welcoming to outsiders.

This failure to reach out to us opened an opportunity for Barack Obama. Because many of us felt that the Hillary campaign was a closed shop, he was an obvious second choice. I was invited to have dinner with him one on one in Washington, D.C. It was a very pleasant dinner and he encouraged me to talk about myself and my background.

◄ THE MONEY GUY

Looking back, I made a very serious mistake. I talked about the positions I had held in various campaigns and at the DNC and DGA. My mistake was in not explaining the role that I played. The job titles did not adequately convey the role. That role was reaching out to fundraisers around the country, meeting with them, bringing them on board and then making them feel appreciated and loved. Because I am not wealthy, in every previous campaign my expenses were picked up by the campaign such as an apartment in Washington or a hotel room plus my travel expenses. I didn't bring that up with him but his finance director told me later that the campaign had decided not to pay expenses for anyone.

I had written a letter to 400 of the top fundraisers in the country and had received positive replies from about 100 of them. I gave the leads to Obama at dinner. But unfortunately I was never asked to be involved after that and I couldn't afford to move to Chicago on my own dime. He had already decided to make Penny Pritzker, a member of a prominent and very wealthy Chicago family as finance chairman. I did not know Julianna Smoot, the finance director.

I was impressed with the fact that Barack gave me his cell number and told me to call him at any time. I never did but he obviously understood that this provided a connection which was very personal. I flew to Chicago but I was assigned a little cubicle and was not a member of the leadership team. It was not much fun so I went back to Miami.

When I was calling prospects for Obama, many people asked,

THE FINAL CAMPAIGNS

"Mr. Farmer, what is your role in the campaign?" Major donors expect to develop a relationship with the leadership in the campaign and if you respond, "I'm just a volunteer like everyone else" they would much rather deal with someone else who will be around in the event of success. Because I served as the national treasurer on other presidential campaigns, that title assured them that if we won, I would be in a position to take their calls and lobby on their behalf for a job or an invitation to the White House. Titles do matter. They should not be given out lightly because if the recipient fails to live up to the responsibility of the job, it's a waste.

In reflecting on my fundraising career, I believe that any success I enjoyed came about because I worked fulltime at it. Most people have careers and jobs and their participation is only on a part-time basis. I was in a position to devote full time to each campaign and that worked very much to my advantage. I've always said," The real power in a political campaign is with the person who picks up the phone." Because I worked fulltime, that person was usually me.

My limited role in the Obama campaign made me ripe for recruitment by the Clinton campaign. My friends on the Clinton campaign had never given up on me. On my birthday in September, three leaders of the Clinton campaign called including Terry McAuliffe. Mark Weiner called me all the time. I also valued my friendship with the Clintons and felt badly about being on the other side.

I then made a very serious error in judgment. I switched

allegiances. Before I endorsed Hillary, I felt it was important to let the Obama campaign know, particularly some close friends with whom I had worked on the Kerry campaign. The Obama campaign released the news with its own spin on it. This upset the Clinton campaign because they had wanted to release the news themselves. The story was picked up around the country as ``Prominent Fundraiser Defects from Obama to Hillary''. At that point, the Washington Post called me and asked me to do an op-ed piece explaining my decision. The opinion piece ran on Tuesday, January 8, 2008 with the headline: ``Why I Still Back Hillary Clinton''. In the piece, I explained that I initially did not think Hillary was electable and was attracted to Barack Obama's freshness and message. But as the year went on, I began to worry that Obama might not be able to go the distance and win the election in November. I called him ``still largely untested and inexperienced''. I said I thought she could hit the ground running as president. Remember, I wrote this after he won Iowa and before New Hampshire. The Clinton campaign emailed the piece to their New Hampshire list. The day the piece ran in the Post, Hillary upset Obama 39 to 36 percent, by only 7,589 votes to win the New Hampshire primary.

I admit I made a big mistake. You should never change horses in mid-stream. In politics, loyalty is everything and I violated that principle. I should have gone with Hillary in the first place out of loyalty to our long standing friendship or stuck with Obama. After I publically endorsed Hillary, I expected to be somewhat involved with her campaign but I was never asked. By switching at that critical point, I doomed my relationship with Barack Obama. Somehow I don't expect to be invited to the White House any time soon. To be perfectly fair, the Obama team did a terrific job of fundraising without help from me.

Epilogue

I expressed some concern to my brother Brent that this book might appear to be bragging. My brother immediately responded, "No modest person ever wrote an autobiography." I decided it is impossible to argue with that logic.

My first political act took place in 1944 when I was six years old. I carried a banner for Robert A. Taft, the politician known as Mr. Republican who was running for reelection to the U.S. Senate from Ohio. The following spring, as my friends and brothers and I rolled around in a mud fight behind our house, we learned President Franklin D. Roosevelt had died. I said, "Hoorah! President Roosevelt is dead!" My older brother Sterling said, "Bob, don't say that. He is the President!" I concede my reaction was impudent and inappropriate but, in my defense, I had only heard anti-Roosevelt rhetoric at our Midwestern Republican dinner table. I find it ironic that I later spent decades of my life raising money to help progressive Democrats win the White House. But that also says a lot about our country and its diversity, the promise that is America and the opportunities I enjoyed in my life to grow and learn.

◂ THE MONEY GUY

As I look back on my life at the age of 72, I realize how very fortunate I am. My parents and grandparents made certain that I grew up in a loving environment with access to the best schools in the country. Being able to go east to attend Dartmouth and Harvard gave me not only an excellent education but entrée to people and opportunities that helped me in every endeavor in my life. For example, a friend introduced me to Francis Ouimet, the first amateur to ever win the U.S. Golf Open, when I was moving back to Massachusetts. Ouimet was only 18 years old when he won the U.S. Open at The Country Club in his hometown of Brookline. He sponsored me for membership at the Brae Burn Country Club.

Throughout my life, I met some of the headliners of the 20th century. My friends joke that there has been a Zelig quality to my life and I cannot disagree. I was introduced to former First Lady Eleanor Roosevelt at a student government conference when I was an undergraduate at Dartmouth. I was active in student government and served as president of my sophomore class and treasurer of my fraternity. I remember how gracious she was and how exciting it was to visit with her for a few minutes at a reception.

When I was working for Ernst & Ernst in New York City many years ago, Richard M. Nixon, the former vice president, had just been defeated in his campaign for governor of California and joined the prominent Mudge Rose law firm in New York. I wrote him a note and said I was on leave from Harvard Law School. I described myself as a

EPILOGUE

great admirer and offered to help him with any correspondence he might have.

He invited me to his office and autographed a copy of his latest book "*Six Crises*". I did a little bit of correspondence work for him but soon had to leave New York and return to Cambridge to finish school. What I remember most about him is he looked like an ordinary guy but he was very, very smart and during a meeting he dominated the room. He had narrowly lost the presidential campaign of 1960 to John F. Kennedy and at the time it looked as though his political career was over but he came back and won the Presidency in 1968.

Later while in the honors program with the Internal Revenue Service, I met former President Harry S. Truman. I was attending a conference in Kansas City and went to visit the Truman library on a free afternoon. I asked the receptionist if the former President was around. This would never happen today but he was and he invited me to join him in a replica of the Oval Office. We sat and talked for 45 minutes in two chairs in front of the desk. He did not sit behind the desk but sat with me companionably in a guest chair. I learned something from that. That simple gesture on his part put me at ease and taught me that if Harry Truman could come out from behind the desk to make a young man he barely knew feel comfortable, so could I. I think he was very disappointed to learn I was a Republican.

And, of course later, I had the opportunity to work with some of the most compelling leaders of my time. When I

THE MONEY GUY

``retired" from business in 1983, I had no idea that I would enjoy six more career changes over the next 30 years. Becoming friends with Bill Clinton and being able to help him win the presidency and serve in his administration will always be a highlight of my life. Bill Clinton's charisma and intellect are well known but until you experience it, it is hard to describe the presence he has. He is capable of making you feel as though you were the only person in a crowded room when he speaks to you. The man has an intensity of focus that is truly amazing.

I had the privilege to golf several times with President Clinton. It was always a lot of fun. When Don Van Natta wrote a book on presidential golf called *First Off the Tee: Presidential hackers, duffers and cheaters from Taft to Bush*, he quoted me as saying the game ``doesn't recognize that your first name is Mr. President or not." Bill Clinton always got a raw deal in being described as someone who took the extra shots known as mulligans. It is a misinterpretation of what actually took place. Every time I golfed with the President, it was always a foursome and the local golf pro always joined us. Needless to say, very few golf pros would pass up the chance to golf with the President of the United States regardless of his political views or party. Whenever the President took a bad shot, the pro would put down a second ball and show him what he had done wrong so the President would take another shot. So he was simply being polite and following the instructions of the pro golfer, not cheating.

EPILOGUE

Clinton had a lot of power as a golfer and he could hit the ball a long way. He was always intensely interested in the technology behind the newest golf clubs. But that curiosity was characteristic of his intelligence. He has something close to a photographic memory. The man remembers everything. And he has a keen understanding of human nature as well as extraordinary depth of knowledge of history and foreign policy. I found him similar to Abraham Lincoln in his ability to talk about big issues in simple language that everyone could understand. I know Ronald Reagan is called the Great Communicator but I found Bill Clinton was as good as anyone I have ever met in being able to communicate public policy complexity to the public.

I often tell a story about how one of the perquisites of being a national campaign treasurer is you get the chance to fly around the country on a small private jet with the candidate early in the campaign. I would say that Bill Clinton was always telling a story, John Kerry was always on the phone, Dukakis was always reading a public policy document and John Glenn ... was always flying the plane. I have a photograph that I treasure showing me in the cockpit with Glenn wearing head gear pretending to be his co-pilot. Glenn flew combat missions in World War II and the Korean conflict, was a Marine Corps test pilot and one of the original seven Mercury astronauts. He was a highly skilled pilot and continued to fly his own plane as a private citizen for years.

I have very few regrets. As much as I admire Michael

◄ THE MONEY GUY

Dukakis and felt badly that he lost the Presidency in 1988, I did not fear for the country because I viewed George H. W. Bush as a good and decent man. I did not feel that way when John Kerry lost in 2004 even though I was probably much closer to Mike and Kitty Dukakis personally. I felt Kerry's loss to George W. Bush was a disaster for the United States of America and nothing that took place since that day has dissuaded me of that view.

I am very proud to have played a role in John Kerry's political career. I have great affection and personal regard for him. He is an incredibly eloquent man. I watched him once speak with extraordinary ease and intelligence about the environment to a group of hard core environmentalists in California for 45 minutes without a single note. He does not have the common touch that Clinton has, but he is a person of uncommon principle and morality and he would have made an excellent President.

But my years as a political fundraiser were more than just an opportunity to mingle with famous people. I made lifelong friends with enormously talented businessmen and women and political operatives whose friendships enrich my life to this day. I am particularly proud of the young people I mentored who became incredibly successful. Tony West, my chief of staff on the Dukakis campaign, is now an assistant Attorney General and head of the Civil Division at the Obama Justice Department. When Dukakis ran for President in 1988, a friend wanted me to hire his nephew to be my chief of staff. But Mike Dukakis said no, he wanted

EPILOGUE

me to have a minority group member because I played a visible role in the campaign and he wanted his campaign to reflect the diversity of the country at every level. Nick Mitropoulos, Dukakis' body man who worked for many years at the Kennedy School of Government at Harvard, recommended a young African American who had just graduated from Harvard and was on his way to study at the London School of Economics on a Rotary Scholarship. Tony West agreed to postpone his studies for the summer. He so enjoyed the experience that he gave up his scholarship (much to the dismay of his parents!) and ended up working for me for several years. One day we were arguing furiously on a plane trip about something inconsequential, probably my schedule. When Tony noticed that the other passengers were watching us with some alarm, mouths agape, he looked up at them, smiled broadly, and said, "It's OK... he's my Dad." Tony went on to become the first black President of the Stanford Law Review and a distinguished lawyer in his home state of California and in Washington. Tony is a real superstar and I am so proud that I know him and humbled that he credits his experience with me with his ability to be comfortable in virtually any setting and with people of any social and financial standing.

I also lived in a time of extraordinary advances in public attitudes towards gay men and lesbians. I went from being fearful and furtive about my sexuality to being able to live openly with my partner. While discrimination still exists, I feel fortunate to live in a country and at a time when I can be open and honest about my life.

THE MONEY GUY

Not long after John Kerry asked me to be treasurer for his 2004 presidential campaign, I learned that Robert Novak, the famous conservative and syndicated columnist, intended to ``out'' me in a column. I had been out to my friends for a long time but I was not at all comfortable with the idea of being labeled in a syndicated column. In my role as John's campaign treasurer, I met with many different types of people and did not want my sexuality to be a distraction. I could not assume that every potential donor would be open minded and did not want Kerry's campaign to be hurt by this sort of disclosure. I called my friend Lester Hyman for help.

Lester is a Washington lawyer from Massachusetts who was a protégé of President John F. Kennedy. Lester has acted as adviser to eight presidential candidates and held a number of prominent positions including a cabinet post as Secretary of Commerce and chairman of the Democratic Party in Massachusetts. Les had been Bob Novak's lawyer for 30 years. Lester and Bob disagreed on just about every issue but they were great friends. In fact, many of Bob Novak's closest friends were liberal Democrats. So Lester called Bob Novak and said, ``Look, I understand you are going to out Bob Farmer. I really wish you would not do that.'' Bob Novak said he viewed it as a good story. Lester appealed to him to think about how it would affect me personally and told him that outing me in print would hurt me deeply. Novak thought about and called him back and told him he was right. He never wrote the column.

EPILOGUE

A few years later when I was ``retired" from political fundraising, I assumed a more visible role on an important civil rights issue in my adopted state of Florida as finance chair of Florida Red & Blue, the campaign to fight an anti-gay marriage amendment to the state constitution in 2007 and 2008. Like many gay people of my generation, I had little interest in getting married myself but I felt that it was discriminatory for the state to prevent law abiding people who happened to be gay from enjoying the same privileges as heterosexual people and I did not want discrimination written in the governing law of the state where I lived. We raised $4 million and I traveled the state and met some wonderful people, both gay and straight, who shared a strong belief that sexual orientation should not be a factor in basic civil rights. The campaign was unsuccessful but I was glad to make a stand and I believe that we are on the right side of history on this issue and eventually gay people will be extended the same privileges and rights as everyone else.

Over the years I have gotten to know quite a few high net worth individuals and drawn upon those relationships in recent years to help raise money for some exciting cutting edge start- up companies, including Sober Steering Sensors, a company that produces sensors to prevent drunk people from driving, and Northwest Biotherapeutics Inc., a biotechnology firm that is developing immunotherapy products to treat cancer. I take a lot of pride in being able to follow my Granddaddy's example and still generate enough income from my work on six corporate boards to

THE MONEY GUY

support myself at the age of 72 and as Granddaddy always advised to ``protect the principal''.

But at the end of the day, I must say that the most important thing I have learned over the years is the importance of family and that circle of intimate friends who, as an ethnic friend of mine says, ``would hide you in the cellar.''

I often think of a story involving my mother and my 50th birthday. My 50th birthday fell on September 20, 1988, just six weeks before the presidential election. Michael Dukakis was the Democratic Presidential nominee but he and Kitty found the time to throw a spectacular black tie party for me at a Boston hotel. More than 350 of our top fundraisers were invited. About a month before the party, my mother called and said, ``Wouldn't it be very nice if you invited your cousins.'' I replied, ``I haven't seen them in ten years. This is a political event. I'm not paying for it so it would not be appropriate.'' The next day Mother called and said, ``I woke up last night and decided that you are right; you do not need to invite your cousins. But in that case, your father and I won't be able to attend.'' Needless to say, I invited all 12 of my cousins and they all came. And while I rarely see any of those 350 very important people, I do see and enjoy the company of my cousins. In fact, as I get older, I become even more involved with my family.

Mother had no interest in celebrities. If they did not know her, she did not care to know them. I invited my parents to a black tie reception at Ted Kennedy's house in McLean, Virginia for the John F. Kennedy Library Foundation. I took

EPILOGUE

a lot of pride in being able to invite them to mingle with a bevy of famous, even iconic figures including President Ronald Reagan, Former First Lady Jacqueline Kennedy Onassis and John F. Kennedy Jr. but she had no interest in rubbing shoulders with the famous. When I tried to persuade her to attend the event, she said she and my father were too old but I pointed out that they drove back and forth from Ohio to Florida every year. Then she said,``But we wouldn't know anybody.'' And I assured her that she would recognize some of the most famous faces in America. ``But she said, ``But they would not know us.'' Mother did not relish the idea of spending the evening gawking at a bunch of celebrities. I have to say Mother was always right about that sort of thing. The moral of those stories is you truly only have family and a few close friends. It is easy to become dazzled by the glamour of public life and I certainly enjoyed my time in the sun but I appreciate the constancy and love of my partner, my brothers and other relatives, and my closest friends more every year.

Tim McNeill and I sponsored two Vietnamese brothers who were refugees living at the notorious Pulau Bidong refugee camp in Malaysia in 1979 so they could come to the United States. Thieu and Hieu Nguyen were from a family of eight children in South Vietnam. Hieu was a 28 year old former South Vietnamese Army officer and Thieu was just 16 at the time. Hieu had been drafted into the Army while studying law. After South Vietnam fell to the Communists in 1975, he was sent to a reeducation camp by the Communist government for three years. Life in Vietnam was extremely difficult in those first years after the long war. When the Communists threatened to commit him to another reeducation camp after his initial three years, Hieu decided to escape and took his youngest brother, Thieu, with him. They somehow survived four days and nights on a tiny leaky boat and made it to Malaysia. About half a million of the so-called boat people escaped from Vietnam in the years between 1975 and 1996 while an estimated 800,000 perished in the high seas trying to escape. I will always be grateful Thieu and his brother survived. The brothers lived in the camp for eight months before we were able to sponsor them and bring them to Brookline.

Both boys went to school, married, and built successful careers. Hieu moved out in 1982 to set up his own household and Thieu stayed with us until he finished work on his master's degree in mathematics at Boston College where he earned his undergraduate degree after graduating from Brookline High School. Thieu was able to sponsor his mother and all but one of his siblings in Vietnam and bring them to the United States thanks to an unexpected encounter with then Congressman Chet Atkins during the 1988 New Hampshire presidential primary. During the 1988 Dukakis campaign, Thieu worked on the finance staff of the campaign. When he met Congressman Atkins who represented the 5th district in Massachusetts, Atkins offered to help get the rest of Thieu's relatives to the United States. When Thieu and his brother had left Vietnam in that tiny leaky boat in 1978, they thought they would never see their mother and siblings again.

EPILOGUE

Thieu's father died when he was very small so I became the father figure in his life. Thieu became the son I never had. He traveled with me all across the United States during my political years and I eventually legally adopted him because he was part of my family and my life.

Thieu now holds a senior position at John Hancock Financial Services. He is married to a beautiful woman, Tina, another Vietnamese immigrant who is a lovely person and exceptional mother, and the father of a wonderful son whom he named Robert after me and two spectacular little girls, Emily and Melanie. Melanie was conceived while they visited me in Bermuda. The children call me Grandpa and watching them grow is one of the greatest joys of my life.

As I look back over the last few decades, I marvel at the advancements in technology. During the Glenn campaign, we conducted all business by telephone, postal letter and Federal Express. During the Dukakis campaign, we used the facsimile to transmit information. By the time of the Kerry campaign, all communications were conducted by computer and cellular telephones. Everyone wore a Blackberry or two and e-mail was the way everyone communicated. Needless to say, communications sped up considerably. An issue that might have taken a day to resolve back in the 1970's, was resolved within minutes in 2004. The 24-hour news cycle also changed the way campaigns were conducted and I must say, not for the better. The partisanship and nasty back and forth of cable television has hurt, not helped our country.

◄ **THE MONEY GUY**

I will always treasure the opportunity to serve as U.S. Consul General to Bermuda but I did not get involved in politics for personal gain. I have been no closer to any political figure than Michael Dukakis and I only asked Michael for one thing: to make Dermot Meagher, a brilliant lawyer, the first openly gay judge in Massachusetts. I had known Dermot since Harvard Law School. Vin McCarthy, another brilliant lawyer who helped many people overcome alcoholism and must be one of the nicest people in the world, and I went together to make that pitch to Michael. Dermot went on the bench in 1989 and served with distinction. He is retired now in Florida and an accomplished artist.

I fondly recall some truly hilarious moments. I remember once Lenny Riggio, the chairman and CEO of Barnes & Noble, arrived at a campaign fundraiser in New York City wearing a tuxedo because he was heading to another formal event later in the evening. Barnes & Noble is the world's largest bookseller, a Fortune 500 company. A society matron walked over to us and asked Lenny to get her a drink. She thought he was a waiter. When I introduced him as the President and CEO of Barnes & Noble, she nearly died of embarrassment.

Reviewing my life from the advantage of my 72 years, has given me perspective I never had as a young man. While I have enormously enjoyed every single encounter with every headliner I met in my life, I would rather have the opportunity to dine with my parents and grandparents one more time. Each of my parents and grandparents had

EPILOGUE

vibrant personalities and were people of remarkable ability and achievement. I was blessed to have their example as strong role models.

But, it has also occurred to me that as I get older and my memories fade, to ponder their lives in the overall scheme of things. As one ages it is inevitable that we lose friends and acquaintances who have been part of our lives. What strikes me is that at the end of the day what have we really accomplished? And what do we leave behind?

First and foremost, I believe that everything we achieve and accomplish has been done to make ourselves feel better. If one is a philanthropist, he can affect many lives in a positive manner. When we go to our reward very few will remember our generosity. A case in point is that both my grandfathers and my father were extremely generous to their families. There has been a philosophy in my family that we can spend our income but that the principal should be passed down to the next generation. My granddaddy, Gus Farmer, established trust funds that paid for our summer camps, orthodontics, prep schools and ultimately college and graduate schools. He passed away when I was 16 years old. He had a big impact on my life, but, in fact, I didn't know him very well. From time to time I have seen the question posed: who are the people you'd most like to have dinner with from history? My choices would be my parents and grandparents. With the perspective of my 72 years, I would love to listen to them again talk about their lives.

◄ **THE MONEY GUY**

I'm sure it made Granddaddy Gus feel good to guarantee opportunities for his grandsons. But, despite the difference it made in my life and my brothers, I don't really think about it very much. So.... I conclude his reward was that his generosity made him feel good about himself.

When I read Professor Stephen W. Hawkings' book about the origin of the universe, it made me think about religion. It seems to me that religion has been the cause of most of the wars and many of the atrocities in history. From my perspective, many of the founders of various religions were spiritual people who developed a philosophy of how to lead your life most effectively. This was their appeal. To the extent that their philosophies have been distorted and used by their successors to oppress other people, is a pity and disgrace. And yet, religion can be a positive force. I can recall asking Mother, ``Mom, you and Dad don't attend church and yet every Sunday you dress up the kids and send us to Sunday School. You don't appear to be religious so why send us?'' My Mother replied,``We have many friends who have found great satisfaction and comfort in their religion and we didn't want to deprive you children of the opportunity to have that experience. '' As I grow older, I see the wisdom of Mother's thinking.

When I served in Bermuda, I attended many church services in my official capacity. I found that I enjoyed it. I liked the music and the hymns I remembered from my childhood. I also enjoyed listening and reflecting upon the minister's homily. Thinking upon issues within the context of my own behavior and its impact on the world made me a better person.

But I drew the line at believing that my religion, Christianity, was superior to other religions. I doubt if there is a hereafter (after all it would be very crowded) but hope that I am wrong. I believe that if you lead a decent life and avoid hurting other people and help people when you can that is its own reward.

At the end of the day, I am fortunate to have enough money to live comfortably. Yet, like many people my age, I worry about leaving enough to my son and partner to ensure that they enjoy the life style I have enjoyed.

It strikes me that once someone passes on and is not part of your daily life, they tend to quickly fade from your consciousness. Living always trumps death in that way. Consequently the lesson I take from this is that we each need to take satisfaction from what we do and try to leave the world a little bit better place. (Most of us won't have a national holiday commemorated for us.) It is easy to be blinded by glamour and greed but at the end of the day what matters is love.

I have some vivid memories from my political years: Mike Dukakis' deep love of public policy, his devotion to his wife and his utter total lack of pretention; The sight of Bill Clinton's eyes lighting up when he spots a familiar face and the warmth of his big bear hug; John Kerry's wry sense of humor and his relentless drive to make the world a better place. It was a real privilege to be part of their lives.

A friend asked me the other day, if I would be available if I got a call to become involved in Barack Obama's reelection campaign in 2012. This old fire horse did not hesitate for a second. I replied: ``Absolutely!''

Why would I do it again? I suppose this is my way of fulfilling my own hopes of being a ``great American'' and contributing something to our remarkable democratic process. But I must again quote the wisdom of my old pal Joe Grandmaison: ``to experience a fleeting moment of almost being relevant.''

CPSIA information can be obtained at www.ICGtesting.com
Printed in the USA
LVOW04s1235310814

401724LV00031B/2826/P